# BROKEN CHAINS

Courageous Women Overcoming Obstacles and Living on Purpose

# BROKEN CHAINS

Courageous Women Overcoming Obstacles and Living on Purpose

## RUBY MABRY

# BROKEN CHAINS

Published by Purposely Created Publishing Group™

Copyright © 2019 Ruby Mabry

All rights reserved.

No part of this book may be reproduced, distributed or transmitted in any form by any means, graphic, electronic, or mechanical, including photocopy, recording, taping, or by any information storage or retrieval system, without permission in writing from the publisher, except in the case of reprints in the context of reviews, quotes, or references.

Unless otherwise indicated, scripture quotations are from the Holy Bible, King James Version. All rights reserved.

Scriptures marked NIV are taken from the New International Version®. Copyright © 1973, 1978, 1984, 2011 by Biblica, Inc.™. All rights reserved.

Printed in the United States of America

ISBN: 978-1-949134-63-6

---

Special discounts are available on bulk quantity purchases by book clubs, associations and special interest groups. For details email: sales@publishyourgift.com or call (888) 949-6228.

For information log on to www.PublishYourGift.com

# Dedication

To all the women who have overcome obstacles and shown the world they can survive;

To the bruised and battered women who have felt alone, with no place to go;

To the women who were violated and have felt unclean and unworthy;

To the women who battle mental health issues and eating disorders;

To the women who have faced the loss of loved ones and felt hopeless;

To the women who are running, fleeing to a better life;

To all the women who felt chained, but have set themselves free…

We honor YOU!

# Table of Contents

Dedication ..................................................................... v

Acknowledgments ........................................................ ix

Preface ......................................................................... xi

*Embracing Transition*
Cheryl Sharpe ............................................................... 1

*Grief to Greatness: Overcoming Traumatic Losses of Loved Ones*
Dawn Collins ............................................................... 13

*My Story, My Revolution: How I Became*
Sabah Bissainthe .......................................................... 27

*The Essence of Belonging*
Marlyn Bonzil-Juste ..................................................... 41

*I Saw the Red Flag (But Ignored It)*
Muriel Bissainthe ......................................................... 55

*Victory Around the Corner*
Jamila Khechen ............................................................ 63

*He Made Everything Beautiful in Its Time*
Tyria D. Jones ............................................................. 75

*SOS: Struggle, Obsession, and Self-Care*
Ruby Mabry ................................................................. 87

About the Authors ........................................................ 97

# Acknowledgments

I would like to thank God for health, life, and favor; my family; and all of the coauthors for sharing their heartfelt stories.

# Preface

When I decided to write this book, I was originally going to only share my story, share with the world what I have been through and how I continue to persevere, even though I also continue to struggle with my personal issues.

I realized, however, that I was not in this alone, and that there were so many other women who were struggling, facing health issues, domestic violence, molestation, divorce, lack of freedom, and more. I realized that this book should be opened up to them too, to not only share their stories, but also to help others going through those same challenges and issues see that they were not alone.

You see, as women, we tend to be the nurturer and to want to be strong and solve everyone's problems. But who is there for us when we are down and out and need a shoulder or someone to lend an ear? It is important for us to know that it is okay not to have it all together and that we don't have to put up a façade to be accepted or loved.

In this book, you will hear from eight women as they share their compelling stories of overcoming life's adversities with strength and perseverance. They were once broken but decided to break those chains and not be defeated by what they have been through.

These stories help me to realize that shattered pieces can be put back together. Realize that what broke us then won't break us now. Realize that you should never judge a book by its cover, because you will miss out on its meaning and purpose.

Sometimes God will take you through some things in life in order for you to be a blessing to someone else. We must remember, even in our darkest hour, to have faith and to put our faith in God.

Never question what God has in store for you. He has given each one of us a journey, and every day we come in contact with people who we might impress and affect, whether it be at work, at the grocery store, or on social media.

If there is a message and purpose I would like for women everywhere to get from this book, it would be to embrace who you are; to put your pain to use, because no pain is wasted; and to remember that you are not alone. There is always someone to talk to. No matter what you are going through, your blueprint in this world should be to live your best life and to live with purpose.

# Embracing Transition
## Cheryl Sharpe

I remember sitting at a window, looking out on the hills . . . thinking about my purpose, my gift, my specialness, the reason I am alive. At that point, I had been in California about a year, and my grandmother had just passed away a couple weeks ago . . . and my daughter was born in the same hospital only nine days after her death.

It was about two in the morning; the light from the moon shone on the mountains, but I could not sleep. All I could think of was the dream God had blessed me with. I had lost my grandmother, a lady that had protected me . . . but she came back in a dream, a dream where she said I should work. I still remember the dream as if it were yesterday . . .

When I saw her in the dream, I said, "Grandma, you came back to me . . ."

She said, "Where else would I go?" She told me she had to go and sit next to God now, because she needed to intercede for me. Her time was done . . . and she was with me. She told me I should work . . .

Over the next few nights, I pondered on what that could mean, what work that would be. What type of work would I do? My husband worked eight hours away from me, coming home only once a week. Furthermore, I had just had a baby two weeks earlier . . . I hadn't even started the healing process of my body yet. My grandmother had just passed away and I had been unable to attend her funeral, as it was held in Florida and I was stuck healing in California. I felt like a failure.

How could I have as much strength as she had had? I thought back over our last year together. The beginning of the end came when she had a TIA, which is a small stroke, while I held her in my arms. I had just helped her out of the bathtub when her eyes rolled back and she stopped responding. She was so heavy as I tried to support her; it was so traumatic. I was about eight months pregnant with my son, and no one could hear me because I was in the downstairs bathroom and it was about four in the morning. I knew I was on my own. I begin to pray.

As I held her up, I cried, "Grandma, please don't do this, not now…I know you are tired, but don't leave me." I forgot about me being pregnant. I forgot that I was recently diagnosed with lupus. I just thought of how much she trusted me, to make me her living surrogate/power of attorney, and how it was my job to make sure she had her wishes fulfilled. The one wish that she wanted the most was the hardest: once it came to the point that she needed lifesaving measures, she wanted to receive them only if she would be able to get better. How can you interfere with someone wanting to leave life peacefully, once the reality has come that their time is over? Grandma always told me to make sure that I did the right thing, and once the doctors said there was nothing else that could be done, I needed to let her go.

That intense moment seemed like years, and no one could hear my screams. But once again the calm of the Spirit came upon me, and I was able to cry out to my only help at that time, the almighty God. I prayed to God, not now. Please give me a little longer. No, Grandma, no, Grandma ... not now. As Grandma looked at me with trusting eyes, all I could think was, can she trust me to be able to let her go when it's time? I remember thinking that, on that morning at least, I would not have to know. So Grandma came to, and although she was not really able to speak after the last TIA, which she had on the toilet, we were okay. She was able to receive therapy inpatient for about three months, and after that she was brought home, with nurses in place a few time a weeks. When I went to get her, I knew that she only had a year, but she chose to come home with me. It was an honor to be able to protect the woman who had protected me. I prayed to God, not now. Please give me a little longer.

After she had been home a little under a year, I knew she wasn't getting better, because the smell of death began to be noticeable in the room. I knew what it was from working for years in nursing homes, and also from my clinicals at the teaching hospitals.

On the day she died, when the nurses came, I asked, "Do you all think she needs to go to the hospital?" They helped me clean her and then said no . . . they both said she seemed just fine. I put on some relaxing praise music, told her that her last living sister loved her, and called out some family names, such as her kids, to help her remember them. She smiled and rubbed my belly, pregnant with my daughter, as she always did. I kissed her and began to go upstairs to wait until it was time to change her again.

I really did not understand at that time that my life as I knew it was changing: my past was slipping away, in the sweet memories of my grandmother, my future was being attacked by this disease called lupus, and my present was threatened. I felt so alone, but I had to be strong for everyone that was depending on me. In the end, my grandmother passed with dignity, without me interfering.

Siya Rebekah Nutri was born on July 19 after a twenty-four-hour labor. She was the second baby I would have after I had been diagnosed with lupus . . . Imagine having to be strong enough to push new life into the world after you saw an old life go away so swiftly. I was dealing with my own vulnerability with my lupus diagnosis, then also having a baby, which was considered to be high risk. The last baby, Kaiisen, was developmentally challenged, due to either birth complications or the medication that I was put on when I was diagnosed with lupus. But abortion was not an option.

I remember wondering when God had decided that I was strong enough to handle so much pain, and why he would let me start a new life while I was enduring such a hard loss, at such a traumatic time.

In the days that followed, I ran myself ragged, trying to provide the basics for my children and keep up with the house, upstairs and down. I eventually had everyone sleeping in the same room to make it easier. I started bringing food and things upstairs so that I could watch them at night. Truth be told, I hated walking past the downstairs room where my grandma had passed away; it was very cold . . . I could still smell her, but I knew she was not there . . . She was watching me but she was gone. It just seemed so unfair. My husband Dwaine had been out of work due to a car accident where he got a brain injury, and now he had a job to return to with ADT in San Francisco. I had mentioned to him that I might not be able to do everything on my own . . . we had so many kids, I was bleeding, my grandmother had just died, and lupus was affecting my brain—while he had to be rushed back to work . . . Yeah, right.

I was having long late-night conversations with myself, trying to give myself a pep talk of why I needed it to work. God could not have such a sick sense of humor . . . right? I was justified against any more pain . . . right?

My optimistic attitude was turning into resentment, of how horrible my life was and how much of a failure I was—and on top of all that, my husband had to leave to support our family. I was filled with guilt as well as resentment that my husband was away so often, as I was the reason we were in California in the first place. It was a move we made because I thought it would be more beneficial for my health. When I found out I had lupus, our family of eight moved from Florida to South Carolina, and then ultimately to California, over the course of an eight month period. It was a big deal for us to move away from where I grew up. But my plans to beat the odds failed.

I was in denial that I had lupus. Previously I had been diagnosed as bipolar, and the doctors turned out to be wrong about that, so I believed it had to be some sort of mistake. I began to wonder why I had been so challenged, from when I was a child all the way to the present, with the hardest choices and issues in life. As a childhood sexual abuse survivor and a domestic abuse survivor, the countless mishaps that had happened to me did not break me. They made me stronger ... I was a warrior, right? Yeah right. Until I had kids, and they and my mother had to become victims of what appeared to be a dark cloud that began to follow me ... So I thought.

I was at the store one day when I began to realize I could not remember where I was at. I had the kids in the car and I had wanted to get them something from the store to eat. I had become disconnected from reality, to tell the truth; I was doing what I needed to do as a mother, but I felt as if the whole world knew that I had just moved to California, and that I had lost my grandmother, had just had a baby, and was newly diagnosed with lupus.

I went to the hospital that day after being confused with the kids in the car; that was just too much. I had just taken care of my grandmother while pregnant, and I had always been so strong. I had to make someone aware of what was happening, how was I becoming so confused as to forget where I lived. I was in the hospital for a few days, but it did not help. All I needed was steroids and a little rest, but instead they placed me on psychiatric drugs that I should have never had in my system.

I begin to experience a different type of everyday living. I was very confused. I took the kids out of school because I did not want to have anyone hurt them. I watched our security system at night while they slept, and in the daytime I tried to teach them so they would not get behind. My actions became erratic. I began to not let the kids outside. Dwaine was gone all the time, I had lost Grandma, and I had six kids I had to take care of while taking care of myself. I felt like I was losing my mind.

I started to think that Dwaine had betrayed me by leaving, by going eight hours away at such a time of distress. I was getting in altercations with neighbors who were bullying me, but I thought that it wasn't an issue. I was in battle mode, mommy mode, protection mode. It was my job to protect my kids from any harm, as I did with Grandma, as I did with my mother and brother when growing up.

The weight of that would play over and over in my head. I would look at all my kids, how young they were; at that time they ranged from newborn to nine years old, six in the household. I had to be strong for Dwaine; he was six years younger than me, and he always tried to make sure I was okay. This time I wasn't, though, and I knew it. I was so tired of being in battle mode. I was tired; who would take care of me . . .

I finally had to leave, to make it to Florida, to where the rest of my family was. I told my family that I had to get my kids to safety, and my mother and aunt came and got me. I did not know what was happening. I could not remember my name, my kids; I was so confused. I did not know.

I was a realtor, I was a mother, I was a student . . . but then I wasn't. My life was over as I knew it. I did not understand. I did not know who was for me or who was against me. I panicked. I did not know anything at all; I could not figure it all out.

Lupus was attacking my brain; vasculitis, they call it. I wanted to just cry. My family was depending on me to get the strength to figure it out. I could tell. But I could not even depend on myself.

I was not being attacked because of my lupus, I was being attacked because of my destiny. I could withstand it for myself, but I was becoming weak. Now my family was suffering because of me and the lupus, and because I was stripped down to the reality that I had no type of control over what takes place in life. That when it was time to die, we had to go. I could not control the pain of this world, just as I could not control my grandmother dying or my daughter and me almost dying in labor. All I could do was pray to the Spirit and trust in the safe harness that was around my kids: God's love that had always protected us.

I called out to God again; I needed help. I retreated into my head . . . This has always been my survival technique. But this time I could not differentiate what was the voice of God. I could not hear it. I literally laid in bed for six months and went from hearing God's voice and believing that he loves me to not being able to utter his name . . .

That is when it happened. My mind began to play like a movie. I began to see how God was with me when I was a young girl and was sexually abused; I saw his hand in the placement of me in the House of Hope; he covered me. When I was seventeen I broke my neck, and they said I would never be able to walk again, but God was with me. I saw God in my mom being by my bedside for three months, encouraging me. I remembered when my first husband beat me, ran me into oncoming traffic, and held a gun to my head. The counselors that helped me get away—that was God helping me. I began to see that at each level of my life, when I felt like I could not make it through, God was there. Even now, as I deal with my diagnosis of lupus, and possibly MS as well . . . God is with me. There is something amazing about how God's love can engulf you.

Life has so many twists and turns, hurts and disappointments, but it also has angels that are hidden in plain sight, who are working on behalf of his people who feel hopeless. I have always had someone that was a representative of God to counteract the bad.

I am so amazed at the resilience that you can build from being thrust into a lifestyle that you were chosen for. I was told that God makes no mistakes. I am here to tell you today that you are able to go through anything, even things you think are meant to break you, if you just look for the people that were put around you who represent God's saving grace.

As I now face life or death issues, just like my grandma, I can see how she was able to be at peace during her time of transition. In all reality, I truly think that watching her pass away so peacefully allows me to be able to know that, no matter what happens in life, God is with me. As I battle my own illness now, where I am not sure if I will be able to take care of my family, all I can do is know that the same God that took care of me then will take care of me now.

I always think that I was challenged the way I was for a reason. I am proud to say that even with all the doom and gloom, my life is still showing how great God is. Just as God sent me signs to show me that he is with me . . . I can tell you that he is with you.

My journey is still continuing, and it is not easy, but every day, I look and see new angels that God has put in my life. I see new assignments for me to accomplish and new blessings that were designed just for me.

I am afraid not of what will come of my life if I die, but of what will come of my life if I don't live. That scares me more than anything. What would have happened if I had believed my diagnosis from the doctor telling me I would never walk again? If I had given up or given in to the pain when my grandmother died? The trauma alone almost killed me.

We all have a small voice inside that I believe is the voice of God. It is always reminding us that we are able to live this life, not merely existing, but actually understanding that we are built with the resilience inside us to keep going.

I sometimes even now think about my grandmother and her peaceful death, and how she rubbed my pregnant stomach to say goodbye. Even in that touch, my grandmother was an angel for me ...

I remember when I laid in that bed, sometimes not even getting up to eat ... and God showed me the angels that were in my life. I could no longer say, woe is me. I had to say, get up, Cheryl, get up.

I got up, and I began to see the best part about laying in that bed and paying attention to my hidden and seen angels: I came to the realization that I am also someone's angel, and someone is waiting for me. Get up!!! After the reality that God loves me, life is the best. And I am special, with all my unique flaws and amazing reality. I am loved ... just the way I am: a little girl who was sexually abused, a woman who endured domestic violence, a granddaughter who lost her best friend, a mother who just got tired, a lupus survivor ...

I stand before you today as a woman that says, I am a survivor, a warrior . . . in the words of my friend, I stand before you as *ezer*—a powerful, strong rescuer and ally.

Yes, I am working; it's a little different, not in the usual way, with what God has placed in my life, but I am doing it. Please, no matter what comes your way, remember three things: 1) We are always on God's mind. 2) Where there is a problem, there is always a solution and an angel. 3) If we just help someone else, I guarantee, our problems will not seem that huge.

I am not what life has dealt me; I am the solution to the problems of other women and men. I am a solution.

You are a solution . . .

This is what Grandma meant when she said work. And every time I think of that last dream of her, it allows me to see that I am loved.

You are loved, we are loved . . . we are solutions.

# Grief to Greatness: Overcoming Traumatic Losses of Loved Ones

Dawn Collins

I am living a life that I could have only imagined and am filled with gratitude. Through continual growth, I have discovered true inner peace and happiness and am now at a level where I can financially provide for both the needs and wants of my family. Professionally, I am a proven leader in the healthcare industry, with over fifteen years of experience successfully implementing various programs and technologies. My career path has allowed me to become certified in the development and implementation of one of the largest healthcare software systems in the world. I am employed by one of the largest information technology firms in the United States and have worked in top health systems alongside some of the brightest and most innovative technology and hospital leaders. To solidify my expertise in the healthcare industry, I am actively pursuing my doctoral degree in healthcare administration. To fill my passions, I dedicate time to coaching others to grow in their own lives.

At this point in my life, I am confident that greatness lies ahead and I am wholeheartedly in love with my life. But life was not always as wonderful as it feels at this very moment. The truth is that, from an early age, I experienced significant challenges, living through the traumatic loss of multiple loved ones. Although loss and grief are very natural parts of life, grieving led me to ultimately be in a very dark place for a prolonged period of my life.

I know some people that have been fortunate enough to have never experienced the loss of a loved one. But unfortunately, I was not dealt that card. Loss and grief have been a part of my life for as long as I can remember. Some of my fondest childhood memories were summer vacations visiting my paternal and maternal grandmothers. But, while I had wonderful relationships with both grandmothers, I never had the honor of meeting either of my grandfathers. They both had passed away prior to my being born. I had not physically endured their losses, but even as a child I felt a gap in not having them in my life, and I mourned. This gap made my first real brush with loss even more traumatic and difficult to manage.

In the fall of my fourth grade year, I recall sitting in my room and hearing my mother scream. I ran to find her and, as tears rolled down her cheeks, I learned that her mother, my grandmother, had passed away. Four days later, before we could bury her, my grandmother's only son, my uncle, also passed away unexpectedly. We all believed it to have been from a broken heart at losing my grandmother.

My last memories of my maternal grandmother and my uncle were unfortunately created while sifting through their belongings in their homes in upstate New Jersey. My grandmother's quaint home smelled of a mix of her sweet smell, cedar, and mothballs. It felt dark in her absence and was filled with memorabilia of my mother, my uncle, my siblings, and the rest of the family members that had meant so much to her. I cried uncontrollably and only wished that I had been given more time with her and my uncle. Their losses stung. How could we manage not one, but two losses so close together?

My middle school years were no different, as I also faced the devastating loss of my favorite uncle. He was a free-spirited, trash-talking, native Baltimorean man that I adored, to say the least. He always encouraged me to speak up and be a force to be reckoned with, yet also made it his mission to always tell me I was his favorite niece, beautiful, strong, and a southern belle. Additionally during middle school, for the very first time I experienced the loss of a close childhood friend. I had been away at summer camp and returned to be informed by my parents that he had been ejected from a vehicle and passed away instantly. We had just had a conversation on my front steps before I left for camp. I was devastated.

High school also proved to be difficult, with the loss of one of the most important men in my life, my godfather. I recall hearing the pain in my father and mother's voices as they gently informed me of his passing. He had meant so much to me and his loss was unfathomable. I felt empty. I cried. I stopped talking for a period of a few weeks.

As if the pain of the prior losses had not been enough, after nearly two years to the day of losing my godfather, I lost my own father. I was a nineteen-year-old, blossoming academic scholarship recipient in my sophomore year at North Carolina Central University when I received the dreaded call informing me that my father had been hospitalized. He had a minor boil on his leg that had rapidly become infected within the matter of a week. My father made progress during the initial week of his hospitalization, but ultimately his infection spread aggressively to his organs and he was transitioned to an intensive care unit. It was difficult seeing my father, someone I loved and admired so much, literally deteriorate before my eyes.

Throughout the process, my family and I remained by his side and were present with him as often as the unit visitation schedule permitted. We utilized breaks in the visitation schedule to emotionally recharge our bodies and freshen up. On the eerie-feeling day that my father passed away, my family traveled home during the afternoon break hours, but our break was halted by a call from my father's medical team stating that his heart had stopped. They had revived him, but requested that we come back immediately. We rushed to the hospital only to find the strongest man that I have ever known laying all but lifeless before our eyes.

I was inconsolable. I didn't know how to respond or what to do, but I remember hearing the voice of God telling me, "It is time. Be strong and tell your father it is okay to leave." I did just that. I found strength from within, kissed him on the forehead, and uttered the hardest words that have ever crossed my lips. I whispered to him, "Daddy, I love you. It is okay if you have to leave."

Once visiting hours were over, my family and I departed the hospital. Within minutes of arriving home, the phone rang. My mother answered, then dropped the phone and fell to her knees. My father had passed away. I know in my heart that he knew that we could not stand the pain of seeing him breathe his last and waited for us to depart to pass on. But in the back of my mind, I wondered if I could have done more. Did I hear God correctly? Should I have asked him to fight harder? Was it my fault that he left?

My family was riddled with grief and I saw my mother cry, one of the few times she did in my life. She, being the strongest woman that I have ever known, had always striven to shield me from her tears through all the losses and challenges that she, and we, had endured. As I watched my mother's heart break, my own heart broke as well, and I doubted that I could go on with life without my father.

In the days that followed, I withdrew from college and fell into a dark place. My only solace in those days following his death was being asked to write his obituary and having the opportunity to somehow honor his legacy. So, with tears streaming down my face and pain filling my heart, I sat in the dining room of our home and wrote his last tribute.

The loss of my father proved to be difficult for myself and my family, but I was fortunate enough to have an older brother who stepped in and cared for our entire family emotionally, physically, and financially. He was twenty-four years old at the time of our father's passing. We were only three years apart in age, but he immediately became my father figure and the man that I looked to when I needed guidance for the tough decisions in life. He was my best friend, my biggest supporter, and the man that I knew I could always depend on.

As a professional athlete, my older brother spent a substantial portion of the year on the west coast, but I always knew that he was only a phone call away. He had repeatedly proven that to me through his actions. In fact, when I found myself vulnerable and seemingly trapped in an abusive relationship following the death of our father, he was the man that stopped what he was doing, caught a redeye to North Carolina, and appeared at my door to save me. He was my hero.

It was my brother's selflessness that had always made me admire the man that he had become. But seeing him step up to the plate in such an admirable way following the loss of our father only strengthened our bond and deepened my love and support for him. I wholeheartedly supported his journey through his professional football career, his real estate investing, building his beautiful family, writing a book, facilitating youth empowerment and football camps, and his ultimate moves that laid the foundation for what is now his legacy.

Recognizing all his efforts to support my family and me, I offered up my hand to assist whenever I could and made it my personal mission to repay him and prove to him that I, too, could be a success. So, I enrolled in University of North Carolina at Charlotte, fought like hell to overcome academic probation and graduate with my bachelor's degree following the loss of my father, and ultimately began making major moves professionally. He continually encouraged me throughout my educational and professional journeys, and although he joked with me for wanting to be a "professional student" while holding a full-time job, he was undoubtedly rooting for me as I crossed the stage to obtain my master's degree with honors. I knew that he wanted my success just as badly as I wanted it for myself, and having his support allowed me to feel as if I was coming out of my immense grief from the loss of my father.

In the years to come I was faced with yet another blow. We lost our beloved paternal grandmother, whom we all so affectionately referred to as "Gran." She was my world. I knew she had been sick, but ironically, I never imagined losing her. I remember receiving the call about her passing while completing my second doctoral residency in Anaheim, California. I recall my body became numb and filled with disbelief. But without hesitation, I packed up and flew back to the east coast to be with family and to attend her homegoing service. It was tough on me and again I fell into a dark place.

I began to emerge from the darkness of my grief in early 2014. With renewed confidence and direction, my brother and I entered into a commitment to take ourselves to the next level! He had accepted the role as head coach of a struggling football program at our alma mater in Charlotte, North Carolina—West Charlotte Senior High School. It was his dream to rebuild the football program, to return West Charlotte to its former glory, and to encourage young people to achieve their personal best. I had decided to forego the nine-to-five grind at a local hospital and took my ambitions on the road as a consultant. It was a risky move and I was fearful. But it was no coincidence that my journey landed me in northern California, a place that my brother had known well and where he was able to provide me with tips and resources to excel on my journey. We were both on the fast track to crushing our goals, and life was getting better! Or so I thought.

One afternoon while at work in California, I received a call that my brother had medical complications that caused him to be hospitalized. I immediately stopped what I was doing and was in flight back to North Carolina within hours. I spent the next week rotating with various family members to ensure that he was never alone. On Saturday, October 25, 2014, I spent the afternoon with him, told him I loved him, and departed to run errands for his wife. In the early morning hours of the next day, I received the call from his wife that I needed to come immediately to the hospital. I contacted our family and rushed to the hospital to find a medical team tirelessly attempting to revive him. They were unable to revive him and I watched him take his last breaths. Afterward, I laid on the bed with him, hugged him, and told him how very much I loved him. He was only thirty-eight years old.

The loss of my brother broke my heart into a million pieces. I grieved for his wife, my mother, my siblings, and most painfully for his daughter and son that would have to navigate life just as I had, without a father. My heart also ached for the forty-five young men that looked up to him, not only as their football coach, but also as a mentor and in some cases the only father figure that they had ever known. I was saddened for his friends, the strong men that cried helplessly when I contacted them to inform them of the passing of their beloved friend who was like a brother to each of them. I mustered up the strength to write his obituary and eulogized him at his funeral before thousands who loved him dearly.

The year following the loss of my brother was hands down the darkest and most painful of my life. I struggled with depression and with understanding how such a beautiful soul could be called to heaven so early. I felt that his life had ended before it had truly begun. I questioned God continuously: "Why him?" and "Why not me instead?" I felt that somehow my life was less valuable because I didn't have a spouse or children. I wished silently that his life could have been spared in exchange for my own. I felt lost, alone, and hopeless, and I doubted God.

Knowing the grief that others in my family were experiencing, I smiled in their presence, but silently battled demons that no one knew existed within me. I fought daily to get out of bed and perform normal tasks. I became depressed and reclusive, and refused to burden others with my pain or problems.

For a period, I would receive the occasional call from someone checking on me. But those calls often turned into conversations where the caller shared with me the loss of an elderly relative of theirs that had lived what seemed to be a full life, and seemingly implied that I had grieved long enough. I couldn't fathom within my mind how someone could compare the loss of my sibling, best friend, and father-figure, who was in his prime and was positively impacting the lives of so many every day, to someone who had lived a long, fulfilling life. It was like comparing apples and oranges. Besides, who were they to tell me it was long enough or to imply that my grief needed to end?

As the days continued, I faced the reality that the majority of the promises to support me in my grief were unfulfilled, and the calls began to lessen. I was forced to ultimately come to grips with my traumatic loss all on my own. I struggled with the silence of people who had promised to be there for me, with what I perceived to be empty promises. I began to question the intentions of others, and I allowed their absence to make me feel that the alleged love and admiration that they held for my brother, myself, and my loved ones were not as sincere as I had imagined.

Perhaps the most defining moment that I experienced while grieving was when I finally had the courage to request support from a family friend. Their response to my request for help was, "I can't call you every day for the rest of your life." Those words hit me like a swift sucker punch in the abdomen, and tears streamed down my face. But I remember telling my friend, "Please don't mistake my tears for being hurt, because they are a sign of my strength." Those were the very words that I needed to hear to make me recognize that I needed to change the way that I grieved. It dawned on me at that moment that I was responsible for how I grieved and how my grief would impact my life. I had two choices—I could either wallow in my grief or I could use my pain to empower me. I knew that I needed to give myself permission to live again. And so, my journey from grief to greatness began.

I wish I could tell you that there was a magical solution to overcoming the obstacles of grief, but there isn't. Rather, it was hearing someone articulate to me that they could not, would not support me that was my turning point. I realized at that moment that even though my life had been plagued with traumatic losses, God had given me strength to make it through life's challenges. I understood at that moment that God had never abandoned me. In fact, God had been preparing and continued to prepare me emotionally, spiritually, and physically to deal with every battle I faced within my life. Those words revealed that all the support and strength that I needed was right there inside of me.

I made a conscious decision from that moment to fight every negative thought that entered my mind. I prayed incessantly and would recite my favorite childhood Bible scripture for strength: "Fear not, little flock; for it is your Father's good pleasure to give you the kingdom." Luke 12:32 (KJV)

Those simple yet powerful words constantly reminded me that I could proceed without fear, worry, or doubt in all things, because God had armed me with all that I needed. I felt as if I was equipped with the tools necessary to overcome my obstacles and that I alone owned my daily outcome. I began to place all my trust in God.

Slowly, arduous morning tasks such as getting out of bed became an opportunity to thank God for his grace and mercies and to rise with purpose. I began to see the blessings afforded to me through the traumatic losses in my life. I realized that although I had lost loved ones, I was fortunate to have experienced and shared love of such magnitude. Sure, I would always miss my loved ones, but I was armed with God's promises and the love of those I had lost. So, I gave myself permission to live a full and happy life.

The answer to solving my long-lasting grief came in my ability to change my mindset and to hear that small voice within me that reassured me that I was courageous, strong, and capable of all things. I had sat in my sadness for so long that my fears overpowered my strength. I had focused too much on others not calling, instead of recognizing that some of them were struggling silently with their own grief from the same loss. I had become so consumed in feeling sorry for myself that I lost sight of the goodness surrounding me. Rediscovering my strength meant that I could recognize my flaws in healing and abandon the acts of self-sabotage that I had committed against myself throughout the years.

Realistically, I know that life will likely force me to again endure grief at some point and I will continue to face challenges in my life. But having survived the darkest times in my life, I learned that overcoming obstacles, whether they come from grief or from something else, is a matter of never losing sight of the courage and strength that resides within you. Losing a loved one or facing any challenging situation is a matter of having the will to see that there is always a lesson to be learned and a reason to be grateful. Focus on the positive that surrounds you, practice a continual spirit of gratitude, and always face life tenaciously in all that you do!

# My Story, My Revolution: How I Became

## Sabah Bissainthe

Life does not always work out as we plan. The constant ebb and flow of circumstances often dictates the direction of our life. That is how it was for a young man with a wife and four children who felt stuck in a war-torn country in the Middle East. He wanted more for himself and his family. So, he embarked on a journey for a better life, a journey that landed him in Liberia, a small country in West Africa. He left his wife and children. It would only be for a short while, then he would send for them. At least, that is what he envisioned. But weeks turned to months, months turned to years, and the years evolved into two extramarital relationships and three additional children—two girls and a boy. One of those girls was me. Hello, my name is Sabah Bissainthe, and this is how I became.

I am a product of a biracial, unwedded, and mixed religion relationship, a relationship that was and still is considered forbidden in my father's culture. My father grew up in a culture and environment where marriages were arranged and men could have multiple wives; an environment where the women covered up from head to toe, school was not for girls, and the girls were raised up to be domestic women without voices of their own. He moved to an environment where men could have wives and mistresses, school was for all but not all went to school, and your upbringing was defined by your parents' morals and belief system. So, it was no mystery to me why I was confused. I saw three worlds: the world I was born of (my parents of two separate cultures and belief systems), the world I was born into (the country of Liberia), and the world I was raised by (my father and my stepmother).

Liberia was, and still is, a country that accepts all. How you raise your family is your choice. You either become the product of your environment or the product of whatever choices you make in life—if you are free to choose. For a while I was the product of my environment. When I was three years old, my stepmother (who I fondly called "ma") joined my father in Liberia. She was the full-blown product of her environment. She was raised to be domestic, did not go to school but was darn intelligent and savvy in her own right, and married my father through an arranged marriage. My brother was not even a year old when she arrived. She accepted us and raised us as her own. My ma was a tough woman and a force to be reckoned with. She stuck to her Islamic faith but never forced it on me. Well, maybe just a little. She clothed me in dresses with long or mid-length sleeves and with hemlines that dared not go above my knees, as well as shorts beneath my dresses. She was strict, stricter than my father. My biological mother died when I was five years old. I never really knew her.

Life seemed to be going right along. Then, at around age eight or nine, my life took a drastic turn. My two half-brothers arrived from the Middle East. They must have been in their mid-twenties. Acceptance was not their strong suit. They were also strong forces to be reckoned with. Disdain showed on their faces and the tone of their voices was cold. There was no winning them over. At least, not yet. You can't blame them. Their father had had two affairs. And now their mother was raising two children who were not her own. Tension was high.

To keep peace in the home and to give my half-brothers time to grow fond of us, my little brother and I were shipped to a boarding school which was an hour or so away. My little brother was eventually sent back home. He was only six years old and too sickly. I stayed. My father asked one of the older girls on campus to be my "play ma" or "mission mother" for a small fee. She took me home with her on breaks since I could not go home yet. I don't remember if I ever went home for breaks, but I do remember going with my play ma to her home. Her family was nice. Her brothers spoiled me. They played fun games.

I was nine years old when my father enrolled me at this church-based boarding school. There were others there my age, so it was not all bad. Unlike me, though, most kids were there because it was deemed a good educational foundation for children. I was there for a different reason. The students there came from far and near. My father and ma visited just about every other week. It was always good to see them. I looked forward to their visits while patiently waiting for my half-brothers to be okay with me and accept me.

During my third year at boarding school, in 1979, my life changed again. It started small, when my half-brothers came to visit. They started to accept me. Then, my father unenrolled me from that school and enrolled me into another church-based boarding school, one less than an hour away from home. I am not sure why he did that. One possibility is that there was a riot in Liberia in 1979, and maybe my father, a small businessman, wanted me closer. But at that point I was getting along better with my half-brothers, so I could have gone home. Like I said, I never understood why. Then, in April of 1980, there was a coup in Liberia, during which time the president was overthrown. My father's business was affected.

Meanwhile, on campus, I had fallen and dislocated my right elbow. I was taken to the nearest hospital, where a cast was put on my arm. I don't remember it being x-rayed at all. I watched as my arm swelled up in the cast. My father was not notified in a timely manner and was angry when he arrived at the hospital. He demanded for the cast to be removed. My arm was so huge that it freaked me out. It was a mammoth compared to my other arm. My father was angry with me for not asking them to notify him as soon as it happened. He was angry with the hospital for their incompetence. He was angry with the school for not notifying him right away. I was eventually removed from that school. I was taken to another hospital in the city of Monrovia for surgery, which turned out to be a botched-up procedure. I have never been able to fully bend or straighten my arm since that fateful day. Moreover, I have the ugliest surgical scar on my elbow. After recovering from surgery, I was subsequently enrolled in a local school. It was a Catholic school, and that is where I finished my elementary, middle, and high school years. I was done with boarding school. I was home now.

My brothers had been immersed into the Liberian culture. They hung out with other Liberians and dated Liberian girls. My ma, on other hand, endured backlash from her so-called circle of friends, whose husbands did the same thing my father did—but they chose not to raise those kids. I heard their hurtful comments as they questioned my ma why she was wasting her time with us. "She will be like her mother and shame you." Like my mother? How? Oh, they meant unmarried with children. "Send her to her mother's people, but keep the boy." "Why do you send her to school?" I despised them and vowed to prove them wrong and make my ma proud. My ma ignored her friends and raised my brother and me. I was often reminded that she did it out of obligation and not love. Obligation or love, it did not matter to me. She and her sons accepted me, and that was all that mattered to me.

Then it happened. My parents caved under pressure. I was pulled from school to stay home and be domestic. After all, school was not for girls. But I made good grades. I was a good girl. I even skipped fifth grade because I performed above grade level in fourth grade. I figured if I worked hard, it would give my parents some bragging rights. Boy, who was I kidding. I cried and pleaded to go back to school. I secretly sent letters to my teachers and the principal, asking them to plead on my behalf. My efforts were futile. I became angry and I started to plot my revolution. My plan: run away. That is what I did. It was transitory, though, because my father searched for me and found me. My little brother knew where I was, so he led my father right to me. It may have been transitory, but my message was clear: Send me back to school. I went back to school.

I endured so many things at home and at school. School was my refuge at times. I envied a lot of my friends. They did things I dared not attempt. Their friends could visit them. They could be as fashionable as they wanted. They wore makeup. The closest thing to an adornment that I could dabble in was jewelry and nail polish. But life went on and I persevered and dealt with many things. I dealt with being groped, taunted, and molested. But I endured it by suppressing it all. I was free to live, but not free to choose, so I became the product of my environment for the time being.

I graduated high school in 1987 with a great group of tightknit friends. A year later, my parents were making plans to take a sabbatical back to the Middle East. It had been years since they visited. My father had worked hard, having to start over a couple of times. It was time to go back and rest a while. But I was not about to go on that trip. I was plotting my own adventure. I was going to go to America. So, in early 1989 my parents went on their sabbatical, without me.

My environment no longer defined me. I was now in charge of my destiny. Then, on December 24, 1989, my life would change again. Liberia's civil war began. We all thought it would be over rather quickly, like the coup of 1980. Little did we know that we were in for a rude awakening. The war, which was led by a rebel faction, continued. People began to leave gradually. Food was in short supply. Curfew was instituted. One thing was certain in my mind: I had to either leave or end up like one of the dead bodies on the side of the road being feasted on by stray dogs—or end up as a rebel's sex slave, passed on from one rebel to the next. The realization shook me to my core. I had to leave.

I needed to get to the eastern border to enter the Ivory Coast. Destination: America, land of the free and home of the brave. So, I concocted a plan. You see, every so often a group of people would leave for the eastern border to obtain food and other essentials. My plan was to dress in a manner that would let me blend in with the women who frequently made those trips. I confided in my little brother and shared my plan with him. He knew that the current state of our town, let alone the nation, was not conducive for young girls and women. He found a duffle bag that had many compartments and brought it to me. We hid my passport in the most inconspicuous compartment. I packed very few items. We said our goodbyes and I waited.

It seemed like an eternity, but the momentous day finally came. I plaited a few big braids in my hair, donned a borrowed lappa, or wrapper, a traditional outfit, around my ninety-five-pound-soaking-wet body, and with a heavy heart I headed to the meeting spot where we boarded the bus. Life would never be the same. I left my brother behind, but he promised to get out when he could. I wanted to cry but I could not. Crying would only bring unwanted attention on me. So, like I have done so many times before, I stifled the urge to cry and suppressed my emotions with every fiber of my being.

The trip that would normally take a few hours lasted for two days. We had to stop at various checkpoints to be searched and interrogated. Even though there were rebels on board the bus, we still had to go through these checkpoints. During one of the stops I was detained for a bit too long. Then George, one of the rebels from the bus, came in and basically told the guy to "let my woman go." His woman? No! That is not true. I don't belong to him. Of course, I could not say that. I stifled the urge to cry and suppressed my emotions, again. My heart sank at the sound of those words—my woman. My knees weakened. My heart raced so loudly that it drowned out the world and the voices around me. I drifted into oblivion.

Is he going to need a reward for ending the interrogation? Are they going to pass me around like a piece of meat? After what seemed like an eternity, a quick tug on my hand snapped me out of my bewilderment and back to reality. It was George, telling me it was time to get on the bus and that we would be stopping overnight in the next town.

Nightfall came, and we had to stop to rest. The ladies offered me food, but I was afraid to eat. I had heard that the rebels cooked dog and human remains. So, I only ate what I could recognize, some cassava that I washed down with some water. I was too nervous to even eat that evening, but I was starving, so I choked it down. It had been a long day. I stayed up for as long as I could. I was too afraid to sleep. Afraid of what might happen if I fell asleep. I laid my head on my duffle bag and fought sleep the entire time. I was so glad to see daylight. Nobody seemed to be in a hurry to leave, though. We were so close to the border. If I had known the way, I could have walked.

By midmorning we were packing up to leave when I spotted George in my periphery. I began to pray. Then he surreptitiously summoned me by using the age-old "psst." I ignored him. He got closer and gestured for me to follow him. I prayed for God to give me Samson's strength as I reluctantly followed him. I looked back, only to see the others getting on the bus. Nobody looked my way. This must be normal.

We entered the nearby house and went into another room, one that had a twin bed that looked like someone had just been in it. The room was dimly lit, with a shimmer of daylight that beamed through the planks that made up the window. He eased his gun down to the floor as he simultaneously shut the door. He began to fondle me as he methodically guided me toward the bed. I fought and begged and screamed at the top of my lungs. No one came, and he must have known that nobody would come, because he was not fazed by my screams or my behavior that showed how much I objected to what he was doing to me. He pushed me on the bed and yanked off my wrapper. I fought, screamed for help, and thrashed around, all the while keeping my knees together. But he was powerful, and he successfully pinned one of my knees down with his knee, then grabbed both my wrists and pinned them down above my head. With his free hand he unzipped his pants and lowered his body down on mine, breathing heavily. I felt him against my inner thigh as he tried to use his hand to guide his way in. Then it hit him. He did not have free access, for I still had on my underwear. He would have to unpin my other leg to fully pull off my underwear. But instead he pulled my underwear to the side and again lowered his nasty body down on mine. Weakness overcame me. I tried to scream at the top of my lungs but could no longer do so. I began to sob as I felt him once again against my thigh.

As he was about to succeed, there was a loud and startling bang on the door. I am not sure what he thought it was, but he bolted up like a thief who had just been caught, releasing my wrists and the leg that he had pinned down. I sat up fast like a lightning bolt and pulled down my top and grabbed both ends of my wrapper. The bang on the door was followed by a voice full of command informing him that it was time to go. He looked at me and said that I still owed him and that he would get me on the way back. All I could think was, like hell you will. He zipped up his pants, grabbed his gun, and walked out. I jumped off the bed, wrapped my clothing around myself, slipped on my rubber sandals that had come off during the struggle, looked up to the heavens, and ran out to the bus. The women did not look at me. They all looked past me like I was not there. They never said anything, either.

We finally made it to the border and had to secure another mode of transportation to get to the nearest Ivorian town. The Ivorian border was manned by Ivorian personnel. It was no longer rebel territory. I was free. I sat on the ground and waited for the next bus, my freedom bus.

As I waited for the bus I thought of the of the women who had been on the journey with me. They never said much. They had been kind to me, frequently offering me food. I think they knew that I was trying to escape. All of them were the rebels' lovers; not by their choice, I am sure, but a choice they accepted nonetheless. They had to survive. They became the product of their circumstances,

circumstances they were forced into. They accepted the hand they were dealt.

The bus finally came. A kind Ivorian Border Patrol man paid my fare. He also gave me some boiled eggs and oranges that I devoured. I looked to the heavens again with gratitude in my heart. As I sat on the bus, I remembered the terrifying event that had just occurred. George could have killed me. He could have held me at gunpoint and made me succumb to his will. Why didn't he? God! That is why. But I was free now, at least for the moment. I couldn't turn back, but I could look back. It is okay to look back. It helps us appreciate where we are.

I believe that our future is shaped by the different stages of life that we encounter. Choices are often made for us by those who control us or those to whom our well-being is entrusted. They can hurt us, or they can mold us. We can't be upset at the result of the choices they make for us. Until we are free to make our own choices, we have to do what the current situation requires to get to the next level. My circumstances propelled me to make the choices that ultimately shaped the rest my life. The choices we make at the different stages in our life may not always elevate us to the next level, but those choices must be ours and nobody else's. When I was pulled from school for the sake of perpetuating custom and tradition, I could have given up, thrown in the towel, and said "it is what it is." During the Liberian civil war, I could have given up; I had every reason to. At the time, the future seemed bleak and the present situation was hopeless. But I decided to choose a different ending to my situation, even if it meant ostracization or death. I was prepared to accept the consequences of my choices. We have choices, even when we think we don't. Some choices can't be implemented right away, but we have them. We just have to decide to choose how the story will end. Even if our choices bring failure, it is okay. During my escape, there was no time to worry about whether my attempt would fail. We don't choose to fail. If you choose to go for a walk but you trip and fall, did you choose to fall? You can't choose not to fall, but you can choose a better path and blaze your own trail.

# The Essence of Belonging
## Marlyn Bonzil-Juste

*The only guarantee for failure is to stop trying.*
—John C. Maxwell, *Put Your Dream to the Test:
10 Questions to Help You See It and Seize It*

On any given Sunday, you would find me exercising my magical power of slowing down time. You see, as a Mompreneur, it's nearly impossible to find enough hours in a day to juggle my busy schedule, let alone to shut my mind off. However, on Sundays I give myself permission to veg out, however it pleases me. That may come in the shape of not stepping a foot out unless absolutely necessary; claiming a room in the house for myself to catch up on a good read or to meditate; or, on occasion, staying in my pajamas all day long.

My husband of nearly fifteen years and I are both entrepreneurs. Although our lives oftentimes seem crazy, our blessings surpass it all. God has granted us the ultimate task of being parents to two handsome boys, Nathan and Zaïre. We reside in a beautiful corner-lot home of a quintessential suburban neighborhood in Central Florida, an answered prayer. Moreover, we are surrounded with family and childhood friends, great perks when you have little ones to raise. Nonetheless, we do not take life for granted and count our blessings each day.

When I was young, each year my siblings and I would look forward to our summer vacation. That was the time of the year where we would travel to the US and spend our entire summer break in New Jersey with family. One year, however, something was different. It was the spring of 1990, and things had taken a turn for the worse within the government of our home country, Haiti. Our quiet community and Christian school institution were also feeling the effects of the turmoil. Threats were being made by the opposing forces for all schools to remain closed during their rallies and boycotts. As summer came along, our routine family tradition was upon us, which we all looked forward to. That summer, though, our destination was changed to sunny Orlando, Florida. You see, my mother's parents and closest sister had relocated earlier that year from New Jersey to the sunshine state. Even as anxious as we were as to what this new city was going to be like, we had no idea of what was waiting of us. An essential part of our childhood experience was on the verge of being rewritten.

To say that everything was different would be an understatement. Unlike New Jersey, the city of Orlando was missing a few things that we were used to when traveling abroad: the kids playing outdoors, the corner stores, the sound of diverse Caribbean music from adjacent neighborhoods, and, most importantly, the friends we had made during our previous summer visits. As my older brother, younger sister, and I were having to embrace this new normal, we convinced ourselves that things would eventually get better. Even at such young ages, we were determined to make the most of our vacation and build enough memories to go back home and share with our classmates.

However, to our surprise, our parents broke the shocking news to us: This time around, we would be staying for good in the US. It was clear that my parents were fed up with the governmental issues and lack of security in our country and felt an obligation to protect us. Imagine leaving your own bedroom, only to now be sharing a room with your siblings at a relative's house. Imagine leaving childhood friends behind, not having the chance of saying goodbye or of playing one last game of *la ronde*. Imagine being fluent in two languages and being among the top of your class, only to now have to learn a third language, acclimate to a new culture, and adapt to a new school system. Imagine being so young and having to restart the quest of belonging . . .

Although things were difficult, I forged on ahead until I made a breakthrough. After a gruesome process with the Orange County public school board, my high grades paid off and the green light was granted. My educational background from Haiti had equipped me well enough to be able to skip two middle school grade levels and enter high school at the tender age of twelve. I can still remember the "excitement" that came with the first day of school. Visualize a small, petite young lady, wearing a skirt and stockings at a public school. You see, my siblings and I had attended private institutions all our lives, so our conservative family saw fit that we would continue to carry the same image, even at a school environment that was totally different than what we were used to.

Surviving the first nine weeks was difficult, but finally the constant stares from opinionated teenagers, and my getting lost around the school campus, which felt like a maze most days, began to subside. I met some amazing individuals of Haitian descent who took me in and taught me the ropes, many of whom I'm grateful to still have as friends to this day. A routine had been established, and I actually started to enjoy being a freshman.

I was ill-prepared for what was ahead. My first progress report was issued. Knowing that I had worked really hard to be where I was at, I was pleased to have earned all Bs. I remember the overwhelming feeling of having conquered so much in so little time. I was certainly on my way to maintaining honor roll that year. But things abruptly came to a stop a week later. It was a day like any other until I was asked by my second period teacher to go to the guidance office. What came out of my counselor's mouth that morning felt like a ton of bricks. With tears flowing from my eyes, I was handed a letter to take home, simply stating that I didn't belong in high school. The school board informed us that they had made a mistake by letting me enroll in a high school grade level at such a young age. Despite how well equipped I had been and the maturity I'd displayed so far among my classmates, they concluded that I didn't fit in. The next few days consisted of several visits to the school board office. We met with different administrators and pled our case over and over. At the end of that week, which felt like WWI, they agreed to meet us halfway. Instead of the original arrangement, where I was allowed to skip two grade levels, I was only able to skip one. Meaning I had to withdraw from high school and be immediately enrolled in eighth grade, in middle school.

It was the worst school year ever! I hated middle school with a passion. The students were loud, obnoxious, and mean, and had to be constantly reprimanded by the administrators. The teachers were overwhelmed, impatient, and unapproachable. For the first time ever, I was picked on for the way I dressed, my accent, and anything else that those little monsters felt was unfamiliar to their world. I prayed for the days to speed up, while working to maintain my head above water.

My new living arrangement was crowded. While I was enduring what felt like unnecessary adversity in middle school, things took a downturn at our "new" home. It's one thing when you are visiting family members with an expectation that you are only there for a couple days. It's a whole different ball game when you arrive with a one-way ticket and no specific date as to when you would leave. My aunt, who had become a young widow a few years back, had already been sharing her new home with her two kids and her parents. Space quickly became a concern. My two siblings and I shared a room. Although we would often reminisce about our individual spaces and beds back home, we never complained of the lack of such. Shortly after our arrival to the States, our parents had to return back to Haiti to start working on arrangements to fully transition to the US. It was then that I began to understand how good we had had it. My parents had always had helpers at the house, including live-in ones, who assisted with our chores. In Orlando I was having to acquire cleaning and survival skills. We were fortunate enough to be living with relatives, but even they would get fed up with our "extended stay." We often clashed with the new house rules and felt the absence of our parents, but were reminded that we were only there out of circumstances. We were just kids, but even then we were wise enough to accept our temporary situation and hold on to the promise of reuniting with our parents in the near future. My siblings and I never formally made a pact to withhold any hardship we faced during that time, but neither did any of us ever hint at any of what was going on when our folks would call to check up on us. I grew a thick skin, which helped me to defy the pain of not belonging.

Over the next couple of years, my parents made several trips to the states to come visit us, alternating between themselves. Each time they would head back to Haiti, it would feel like my world was going to end. I clearly recall one particular trip that my mother took during that period of time where I was determined to put an end to my misery. On the day of her departure, I gathered all my belongings and was ready to leave my two siblings behind. The thought of being separated from my parents and treated as an unwanted guest, as well as the loss of the comfortable lifestyle I was accustomed to, no longer made sense. I wanted to go HOME! With tears flowing from her eyes and mine, my mother held me and reassured me that we would soon be reunited. Even at that very dark moment, she only read the unspoken plea for help through my eyes. After all, I was living with my grandparents and aunt; I didn't have the leisure of crying over spilled milk, nor of processing the thought of being a misfit.

At last, there was a light at the end of the tunnel. Finally, the day had come! My parents and my youngest sibling made it to the US, this time to stay for good. A few months later, we closed on our first property in the States and we were back to living under the same roof. After having endured much hardship and emotional abuse, our family was reunited and things were back to normal.

Shortly after, I completed my junior year of high school, and that summer I landed my first real job, not counting babysitting gigs, as a cashier at a local drug store. It was great. I had an awesome management team and a great schedule which didn't interfere with my schooling, and my job was within walking distance from our home. I started training, but on my second week was sent home. That evening, the assistant manager called me into his office, embarrassed. He told me that the hiring manager had been so blown away by my level of maturity and interpersonal skills that they had overlooked the fact that I was only fifteen years of age. It was déjà vu. Unbeknownst to me, the state laws at that time required employees to be age sixteen and up. I couldn't believe my ears. I was immediately taken back to my prior ordeal with the school board. Once more, I was faced with being out of place. My maturity and tenacity weren't enough to supersede any systematic rules and regulations that were in place. Instead, I was left feeling like I was being punished for displaying such qualities. Nonetheless, I didn't dwell on my disappointment. At least this time around I would get to come back a couple weeks later, after I turned sixteen.

Upon graduating from high school, I immediately started taking my prerequisite courses at a local college. A good friend of mine, one of the "pioneers" who helped me throughout my experience in high school, approached me about what would be an experience of a lifetime. Knowing that we both shared an interest in science, she informed me of a private school that she was recently accepted into. The only caveat was that it was located in New England at an upstate city named Lancaster, Massachusetts. I immediately connected with a recruiter and completed my application and other requirements. Things were moving fast. Upon receiving my acceptance letter, I had less than three months to move. Everything was going smoothly. My boarding arrangement at the dorm was finalized; I even landed a scholarship to cover part of my tuition. Besides being apart from my family, life was good. Lancaster was a small, quiet town, mostly made up of the school campus and two local churches. I made new friends who became like family and we began to look after each other. The environment was perfect for someone like myself. Besides the harsh winter months, Massachusetts has one of the most beautiful changes of season; the fall is to die for. By being on campus, distractions were nearly eliminated. My studies were the most important thing for me at that time. I was truly grateful for such an opportunity and was not going to take it lightly.

I made it through my first semester. The cafeteria food, my dorm roommate, and constant studying became my new normal. Summer was coming to an end, and the fall semester was upon us. This was a very nerve-wracking period. Both returning and new students were flocking in the halls of the registrar's office to get clearance for classes. The news I was about to receive was unforeseen. I did everything on my end, during that first semester, to ensure that I stayed within compliance, to keep my acceptance intact and my scholarship active. Once again, though, my defeat was completely out of my control. Being a private college, the school relied heavily on private funding and donations to keep certain programs active that were being offered. That year, they felt short and had to cut off most of their scholarship programs. This resulted in me having to leave the dorm and find other resources to pay for tuition. I no longer felt welcome there.

Imagine getting such news while being nearly 1,400 miles away from home and having no family around. I was devastated. There had been so many sacrifices made to have gotten me that far. I made a promise to my parents: I was not going back home without that degree. That year I was so focused on my path that it didn't matter where I laid my head; I was going to find a way. After pleading with God for days, I was left to remain still, waiting for a new door to open. I recalled specific memories from growing up in Haiti as a little girl, watching the discipline displayed by my parents, day in and day out. My father worked as a field inspector for an international company. Many of his trips would require him to be on the road for a couple of days. He never complained about the gruesome journeys and the obstacles he would encounter while traveling. Rather, he would share with my siblings and me the freedom of being in control of your earnings and would show us his take-home salary. My mother, although having a background in administration, chose to stay at home to raise us. Quitting was never part of my DNA.

Putting on my big girl pants, I quickly learned to adapt. A friend of mine who was living in a student apartment took me in as a roommate. I accepted a job nearby, one within walking distance of the school campus. It only made sense at that time to agree to work third shift in order to not interfere with my school schedule. Little did I know how hard of an experience that would be. Nonetheless, I pulled through and held on to such a schedule for nearly two years. During that time, I purchased a vehicle and transferred to a nearby state university with a more affordable tuition. By the time I reached my last semester of school, I was literally enrolled at three different schools. The hurdles that I'd gone through were not going to stand in the way of me reaching my educational goal and keeping my promise. It was all worth it. During my graduation, I handed my diploma to my parents and thanked them for believing in me and instilling in me the character needed to have made it through the experience.

Using adversity as a catalyst and an eye-opener, I would go on to pursue a graduate degree, making it to a C-level executive position in the corporate world and eventually owning my own consulting firm. There have been many more times where people or circumstances attempted to have me believe that I didn't belong. However, what they didn't know was that my experiences at an early age have more than prepared me to dismiss such attacks and that outside validation was never sought or needed. My anchor was to have faith. It is essential to surround yourself with those who share common goals and to live intentionally. Such will help you to block out the noise and create your own reality where you choose to belong by creating your own narrative.

We often hear that nothing worth achieving is easy. But how can you prepare yourself for the unknown? One of the requirements for attaining ultimate authenticity is to exercise self-love. My simple formula to you is to foster the following top three elements:

1. Preventative Maintenance:
   Keep a balance on your health and wellness journey. Remember the 80:20 rule of healthy eating to exercise. What you put in is what comes out. Seek meditation and prayer at all times to keep a positive mental state.

2. Personal Development:
   Trust me on this, working on yourself won't ever go out of style. The better you are as an individual, the better you can be as a daughter, friend, lover, spouse, mother, community member, etc.

1. Be Openly Vulnerable:
   Being openly vulnerable is the only way you can allow yourself to let go of any stigma or expectations from others. And by doing so, you will reach the freedom to create, as you were meant to, while learning along the way.

The aforementioned sacred keys above can't be achieved overnight; therefore, it's all right if you are not there yet. The point is to be patient enough and to give yourself permission to mess up, get up, grow, and continue to evolve.

Being a business consultant has been nothing short of an amazing journey. And yes, my perspective of my company will always be one that will continue to evolve. I've had the ultimate opportunity to come into daily contact with people from all walks of life. My input and expertise have impacted lives and help businesses grow. I've travelled internationally and stood in front of strangers, from C-level executives to aspiring entrepreneurs, sharing one message: show up authentically, continue to work hard at perfecting your craft, be of service to others, and be convinced that you belong! You should always remember that life has already given you its ultimate gift, and that is life itself!

# I Saw the Red Flag (But Ignored It)
## Muriel Bissainthe

From a young age, my mom always told me to make sure I never let a man disrespect me or make me feel less than the queen I am. Growing up, I envisioned the perfect man, one that worshiped and adored me; we would live a beautiful life, have kids, and live in a house with a white picket fence. Years later, I thought I had met the man of my dreams, my Mr. Right. During our dating phase, he was sweet and loving, always going above and beyond to show me how much he cared for me and for my daughter. He was a hard worker to make sure he provided for us. After dating for five years we became engaged. As we planned for our fairytale wedding, nothing was skimped on; we wanted to make sure that it would be perfect. It was such a happy time. There was no arguing, no yelling. It was a peaceful time.

Days before my wedding, a Category 4 hurricane was coming to town. By a strange coincidence, my new last name was the name of the hurricane. That was my first sign. Then the wedding day itself was rainy, dark, and gloomy. "Doomsday" is what I call it now. The day was a warning of the bad days to come.

When I found out that we would be having a baby, we were so excited. My daughter was just turning ten, and she was happy to be having a little brother.

When my son was born, all of my attention was focused on him. I believe that was when things started to turn bad, as my spouse became jealous of the care I was giving to my son. My days of verbal abuse had just begun. Previously, I had only seen that type of relationship on TV, as my parents had been married for thirty years by then and I only saw love in my home as a child. Life with my husband was much different than what I was used to. He would come in the house and, if he noticed anything as small as a cup on the table out of place, he would begin yelling. "Why is this cup on the table? It needs to be moved!" Other times he would demand attention and disrupt our routine. "Why is the baby sleeping already? Wake him up!" He would wake the baby up, then he would fall asleep, leaving me with a crying baby. It just got worse from there. He began to speak to me like I was dirt under his shoes, like I was beneath him.

When it was time for me to go back to work after my twelve-week maternity leave, it became easier for me to avoid him. After I picked up my daughter from afterschool care and my son from daycare, I would simply avoid going home. I began to stay away from home more and more. I would come home later in the evening and go to my family's house nightly. Whenever he was home the belittling started: You don't know how to do that, it should be done like this! If you leave me, no one is going to want you with the kids, so you may as well just stay! I don't like that food, what did you use to make it, what ingredients did you use? Did you buy this from Publix? You know that's the only grocery store I like! What type of detergent did you use to do laundry? I don't like that kind! The clothes have to be rewashed! I was told constantly that since my family is from the islands, they didn't know how things should be, and that I was not smart enough, even though I have more education than he does.

For years I asked to go to a marriage counselor, but he continually refused. His whole demeanor was that he should be treated like a king and that he was always right about everything, no matter what it was. He had the Dr. Jekyll and Mr. Hyde personality, as at first and in public he was loving, but in private he was so hateful. I was literally cursed out and yelled at about things on a daily basis. I became a prisoner in my own home. There was no way I could live the rest of my life in such a bad relationship. I had to make a decision on what I was going to do for myself and my children.

So many things would go through my mind ... Girl, what is wrong with you, you know better. Why are you with such a person? God doesn't like divorce, but I can't be in a marriage and doing everything myself. My children deserve to see love in their home, and I deserve to be loved and feel love.

I chose not to mention my abuse to my family and tried to deal with it on my own. I was in and out of the urgent care center, dealing with so much stress and depression from the verbal abuse that I received daily at home. Finally, I decided to ask for a divorce.

It was like a wakeup call for him and he agreed to change and get counseling for anger management. It never happened, though...

I was still so hurt and embarrassed, as everyone thought that we were the perfect loving couple. But that was only in public. In private it was the total opposite. Just because someone has the look of having it all does not mean that that is necessarily the case. No one knows what goes on behind closed doors.

I was at my wits' end and at the point of walking away. He planned a cruise as a fresh start to better days. I was hoping that the cruise would help. But following the cruise, he reverted back to the same person.

Weeks after coming back from the cruise, I went to visit my mom. She looked at me and said, "You look pregnant, and I dreamed about fish. Go take a pregnancy test." I didn't believe her, but went to the closest pharmacy to get a pregnancy test just to be sure. My sister, my mom, and I waited a few minutes and checked the stick. It was positive. I was pregnant.

All I could think was, what do I do? Lord, help me... I can't leave him now I'm pregnant.

In the end, it did nothing but prolong the inevitable. Everything came to a head when my oldest daughter was thirteen years old, my son was three years old, and my youngest daughter had just turned one.

I'll never forget that rainy night; the kids were sleeping, and he walked in the house, yelling once again about nothing, really. At that point I was just tired. I asked him to pack his bags and to go stay at one of his family member's house. He started cursing and yelling. He even woke my son up to tell him mommy is kicking daddy out of the house. My son just looked at him. The kids were victims of the abuse just as much as I was. They would hear him yelling and cursing at me. This was not the kind of life I want for my kids.

I want my son to respect women and to never speak to them in a hurtful way.

I want my daughters to know they should never be verbally abused.

But they would never learn that if they were watching it happen to me

I had the locks to the house changed the very next day.

A week later, I received a call from my pastor. He told me that he had gotten a call from my then-husband and wanted to come over with him, just to speak with the both of us, if that was okay.

The pastor arrived with him and asked me what had happened to get us to this point. In so many words I explained, without even telling all of the situations I had been going through; what I did say was enough. The pastor asked him if all of what I said was true and he nodded his head in agreement. He also asked him why should I give him another chance if all of this was true.

The only thing he could say was, "God has spoken to me and I am a changed man."

The pastor asked, "On a scale from 1–10, with 10 being the worst, how would you rate the way you treated her?" He said an 8.

I blurted out, "With everything you have said and with the way you have treated me, one week did not fix you."

I thanked the pastor for coming, stood up, and walked to the door. I wished them a good evening and waited for them to leave.

I will no longer let my heart be trashed like a rag.

I will no longer be a rug under anyone's feet.

I'm good enough.

I'm strong enough.

I'm shining brighter now than ever before.

I promised God that if he pulled me out of this alive and sane, I would help every woman who is going through any abuse; I would go over and beyond to help them. My hope one day is to provide a shelter for battered women and children.

My ex-husband promised me that if I did not want to stay with him, he would make sure that he would never pay me a cent in child support. He has done just that. He sold his business and works under the table for cash. He can keep running, but he will have to serve time with God. I've done my part, being the sole financial provider for my children.

I can only thank my family for loving me enough to help me in my times of need. I hope to encourage others who want to give up and tell them that they are stronger than they think. I want to help lead them in the right direction by telling them my story, of how I managed, with three young children, to leave my abuser, and how I made it and continue to not only thrive but also to be a positive role model. I hope that, in sharing my story, I can help other women find the strength to stand up for themselves and their children.

# Victory Around the Corner
## Jamila Khechen

I was born and raised in Dakar, Senegal, in West Africa. After graduating from high school in Senegal, my mother decided it was best for me to leave Senegal and go to the United States to study abroad. My mother had made all these plans for me to stay and live with her brother. We did not realize that our expectations would have to change when we got to the US. We were not aware that during that time my uncle was going through a divorce.

We arrived on September 6, 2001, in Orlando, Florida, thinking that my uncle was going to pick us up from Orlando International Airport. We called multiple times and didn't get any response back. We were unable to reach him. My mother was starting to worry because we didn't know anybody else in the state of Florida. I decided to take the initiative and told my parents that I had an idea of where my uncle lived, and that we could make our own way there. They thought it was foolish and crazy but didn't have another option. So we decided to call a taxi cab to pick us up at the Orlando Airport.

After hours of waiting, the taxi cab finally showed up. I remember it like it was yesterday. The airport was not busy and very few people were waiting on their ride.

I was able to direct the taxi driver with the little English that I spoke to take us all to my uncle's house. I told him that my uncle was living in Poinciana. I remembered the name of the complex, Fountain Blue. The taxi driver was very familiar with the Poinciana area. As we were getting close to Poinciana Road, I started to recognize landmarks and spotted the CVS. This place was very special to me because my favorite cousin and I used to go there when on a bike ride or rollerblading. It was one of the fun memories I had with my favorite cousin on our first visit to the US in 1998.

As we got closer to the CVS Pharmacy, I told the taxi driver to start slowing down and to make sure to make a left turn immediately. After the left turn, he continued to keep going straight. At that moment, we needed to pay close attention to the signs and names because it was very dark. I was able to recognize Fountain Blue from far away. I was getting excited because we were getting close to my uncle's house. We made a slight right turn at Fountain Blue. My heart started pounding so fast, but I didn't want to show any emotions, didn't want to show that we were lost after that entrance. After that point, I had no idea where my uncle lived. The house was not built yet when we first visited this place in 1998. I started to pray quietly to God to give me a sign.

I started hearing my dad getting anxious. I knew in my heart, though, that God was not going to let us down and that he was going to manifest himself. The streets were dark and it was hard to see the houses. I reassured my dad, telling him to give me a few minutes, and not to give up since we were very close. I got out of the taxi and started walking with my little sister. As we were getting closer to one of the houses, I heard a dog barking. This little voice was telling me, this is it; it was a sign from God. I remembered that my aunt used to babysit my cousin's dog. People might think I was crazy to trust that, but I was so sure that we were at the right house. I started to knock at the door with my faith that it was my uncle's house. I heard a lady asking who it was. I said, "this is Jamila, your niece." My aunt was shocked when she opened the door and saw me with my sister. To my surprise, she asked me what I was doing at her front door at that time of the night. I called my parents over and let them know that I had found the house. My parents felt relief and the nightmare was over. My dad released the taxi driver. The taxi driver gave my dad his personal contact information to keep and let us know that if we needed anything, we could call him at any time.

As we entered my aunt's house, the look she gave us was questioning. We started to ask her why my uncle hadn't shown up at the airport. By the look on her face, we knew something was not right. She announced to us that he was no longer living with them. We were in disbelief. She told us to get some rest since it was late, and she would give us all the details in the morning. She showed us hospitality regardless of what she was going through. In the morning, she made us breakfast and talked to my parents. My uncle had left the house.

My mother couldn't believe that my uncle hadn't told her anything. She discussed with my aunt, her sister-in-law, that she had planned for me to stay with them and go to college. My aunt told my parents that I had come at the wrong time and she didn't think it was a great idea for me to stay with them, since they were not stable. She thought it would be best for me to find a good college and gather all the information needed to stay there.

She took us to Valencia Community College–Osceola Campus. The Osceola Campus transferred us to the West Campus because they dealt with international students. We found a nice lady, Maria. She would be my international advisor and oversee my paperwork. First of all, I had to pass two tests, English and math. I did well on the math part but didn't pass the English part. I missed a passing score by two points. I would have to wait to enroll until after I passed, but my parents wouldn't be able to stay that long. Instead, they would have to send what I needed to enroll from Senegal. Then, after filling out the enrollment paperwork, my parents would have to send a sponsor letter stating that they would support me while I stayed in the US and went to school. My parents hoped that I would be able to stay and go to school like they planned. In the meantime, I had to get better at my English to retake the English section. I was not out of the woods yet. We also had to find me a place to stay. My aunt knew a Portuguese lady that was renting a place near the college. She contacted her and was able to find a place. My parents paid two months in advance to make sure I would be fine after they went back home.

After settling everything, my parents felt they had accomplished a lot in the little time we had. My mother was also finally able to get ahold of my uncle. He was embarrassed and hadn't wanted to let her know that his marriage was failing. My mother asked him to look after me. However, after my parents left, month after month passed by and I didn't hear from my uncle. In that time, I decided to start to focus on passing my English test. I went to the public library and read books. I used subtitles when I was watching TV. I was getting better and making some improvements. I decided to take the test—and failed again. I took the test five times before I finally passed. I never gave up. I knew I was one step closer to my break.

As I waited for my parents to send me the documents I needed so that I could take them back to Valencia to continue the process of enrolling, I started to feel lost. I didn't have any friends. When I was talking to my parents on the phone, I told them that I was doing well, but the minute our conversation was over, I started feeling lonely again and felt the urge to call them back. I had to stop a few times and tell myself that I needed to grow up. I knew deep inside there was nothing in Senegal for me. I had to suck it up and be brave. That made me feel a little better.

My landlord announced that I was getting a roommate and was going to have some company. My new roommate, Sissa, was very nice. She was from Brazil. She knew very little English and was working as a housekeeper. It was nice to have someone to talk to and not just sit looking at the same four walls every day. I was happy. Sissa stayed two months with me and then decided that she wanted to move out. She found another place much cheaper. I was sad and asked her if I could tag along with her. She had to ask her roommate if it was okay. Her roommate accepted and let us share the room, which was great and kept my cost of living down. I was helping my parents not have to send so much money for rent. My new roommate Rose was nice enough to take me to Bank of America to open my first bank account. I was so grateful. She taught me a lot. Sissa decided to move again a month later. I didn't understand at the time why she was moving so much. I didn't realize she was undocumented. I told her that I was going to stay this time and not follow her, because I needed to stay focused and was ready to start college soon.

I didn't realize time was not waiting for me. My stay in the US expired, and I needed to find a solution right away. I prayed every night with no answer. Finally, I decided to go back to the college and talk to Maria. She mentioned that I needed to change my status from having a tourist visa to a student visa. I didn't know anybody who could help. I had lost contact with my aunt as her phone was disconnected. I found myself lost again. But I decided that I was not going to give up, that God had a purpose for me. I started to fast and pray that God would send me an American family to come into my life and help me. God interceded again. He showed up yet another time.

My cousin was traveling through with her husband and I got in contact with her. She was in despair. She told that she was in trouble and needed help. I offered for her to come stay with me. My cousin had a friend from her technical college, and we all decided to go to the beach to relax and take our minds off all the problems. Her friend decided to invite his friend to come hang out with us as well. We went to Daytona Beach and I met this young man. He was a gentleman and he was sent by God. He introduced me to his parents. They were so nice, like I was part of the family already. They treated me like their own daughter. They had always dreamed of having a daughter, but God had given them two sons. They told me that a month before they met me, a lady had prophesied to them that they would have a daughter. They adopted me like their daughter. They asked to be called Pop and Madre. They took me to church with them and we went to dinner together. During that time, things were not going so well with my roommate. I wanted to move out, but didn't know where to go. I discussed my situation with my newly adopted brother. He talked to his parents. They came up with the idea that I could stay with my pop's mother. My adoptive father's other son used to live with her until they lost him to leukemia, and she was feeling alone and needed someone to stay with her. Everything was coming into place. I met my new grandma, and she was the sweetest lady. She was so happy that God had answered her prayers. I had to tell my roommate that I found a place and was moving out. I had one problem less. I had a place to stay.

My only problem after that was changing my status. I didn't know how to address my situation. I summoned up my courage and told my adopted mother that I was in deep trouble. I was out of time to stay in the US and needed to change my status. Since my English was still very limited, I explained to her that she could make an appointment with Ms. Maria, my counselor, to have a better understanding. She did follow up with her, and Ms. Maria recommended that we seek a lawyer's advice. She gave us a number and we called the lawyer's office. We talked to the lawyer and he informed us that there was no guarantee that my application would be approved due to how long my stay had already been. We decided to challenge that. We told him that we were believers and that God had the last word. We were not going to be defeated and were going to pray about it. We decided to fast and pray. We filled out all of the paperwork sent by the lawyer and paid all the fees. With faith, we mailed out everything. After our fast, we got a letter in the mail from the immigration office. I was so nervous I had to ask my adopted mother to open the envelope. She read the letter and my heart was beating so hard that I thought I was going to faint. She sighed a little and said to me: "Ms. Jamila, you are on your way to college." Even though I had not doubted that God would manifest again, I was still in disbelief. It was surreal. I thanked God for another blessing. My dream came true. I was going back to school.

I had to tell my parents the good news and that they should be ready to send me tuition money to start in the fall of 2003. I had one worry still to resolve—how I was going to pay the lawyer fee. So we contacted the lawyer's office and made an appointment. We had to go to the office to finalize some paperwork and pay for the attorney fees. I was shaking so hard. The front desk lady called the lawyer and let him know that we had arrived. The lawyer came out and shook our hands. He was so happy for me and wished me well. He wanted me to succeed and to send him an invitation to my graduation. On our way out, the front desk lady mentioned that we needed to pay the fees. She called the lawyer on her desk phone and asked how much I owed him. I could not hear what he was saying. My palms were sweaty. But then she responded back to me that I did not owe a thing, not a dime. Can you tell that God was there? My God is real. I wanted to dance the holy dance right there in the office, but I kept my excitement to myself and thanked God for performing another miracle. He had set me free from another bondage. I was joyful and on my way to college.

I started Valencia in the fall of 2003. I excelled in college and graduated with honors in May 2005. My journey was not easy, but I persevered during my college years. I never gave up. I have encountered many obstacles because of language barriers, but I made it through at the top of my class. My parents were so proud of me and came to support me at my graduation. After graduation, they had to go back home and I had to continue my journey. I was not done with school yet. I had my associate's degree and needed to go to university to get my bachelor's. I got accepted to both UCF and Florida Gulf Coast University, but I had to pick one school. If I had gone to UCF, I would have been able to stay in Orlando, but I would have had no money to support myself and would have needed to pay for my full tuition. So I decided to go to Florida Gulf Coast University, because I received a scholarship there and they would pay 60 percent of my international tuition fee. I thought it was a big deal to move to Fort Myers, but I had a better chance to succeed there. I decided I had to wait a semester to work and save money to buy a car and get my driver's license, so I requested to transfer my scholarship to spring 2006.

I was able to find a position at Valencia to work as a math lab assistant. I really loved working there. Around August of 2005, I met one of my tutees and she offered for me to go to lunch with her. Over lunch, she told me that the following weekend she planned on giving a surprise party for her oldest brother and I was invited. As we were preparing for the festivity, she asked her daughter to invite her uncle to the birthday party. I was surprised, because I had thought my tutee only had one brother, not two. At the party itself, I introduced myself to the previously unknown brother. He was very nice and liked to joke around. He asked me what I was planning to do with my life. I told him I was saving money to go to school in the spring. He gave me his business card and told me if I needed anything, I should not hesitate to contact him. We started talking and became good friends. He helped me move to Fort Myers and even bought me a dependable used car. I thought it was a blessing. Finally, I had to say my goodbyes to Grandma, as I was ready to move to Fort Myers and continue school. I promised her that I would visit on my breaks and some weekends. As the months went by, I started to fall in love with the man I had met. He started to come to visit me on some weekends and I would come up on my off weekends. We finally decided to get married in September 2006.

I graduated in fall 2007, but got an incomplete in one of my classes. The teacher was so hard with me. I had to explain to her that I was expecting a child. She also did some research and discovered that I had been taking too many credit hours, nineteen hours to be specific. She finally gave me a break and let me complete the course if I finished within a semester, since it was a science project. I was able to receive my diploma in April 2008 and had my son in May 2008, the day after my birthday. All I can say is that God is good and has always delivered miracles, even though I sometimes didn't deserve it.

Today, I have a beautiful family. I have two sons and a daughter. I love to take care of the intellectual individuals that I mentor and help them fulfill their dreams or goals. This was not the path I would have originally chosen for myself; I thought I would be in medical school and become a doctor. But this life has turned out to be something I couldn't have imagined. And like they say, your dream is not dead until you decide it is not important to you anymore. I diligently listen to God and pray that he will continue to guide me. I may not be a doctor yet, but I know enough that people come to ask me for some advice. If God decides I will be a doctor, then I will wait for that day to come, because there is no limitation on dreams. I remember how, the day I graduated from Valencia, this old lady—eighty years old—graduated as well. If she could do it at that age, I am sure I can as well. Never limit yourself or doubt something can be done. Like it says in Matthew 19:26b: "With man this is impossible, but with God all things are possible."

# He Made Everything Beautiful in Its Time
## Tyria D. Jones

Little girls love to play dress-up. One of their favorite things to do is to play house while they're doing so. I remember being that little girl and looking forward to my wedding day. Whenever we were talking about what we wanted to be when we grew up, I would always say I wanted to be a wife and a mommy. When I thought about my "big day," I already knew how I wanted my wedding to look, from the colors to my dress. I've always been the little girl who had to have everything in order. I had a plan that my life had to follow. My dolls even had names, and they were always neatly stacked on my bed or in my room. There always had to be some type of order.

The thing is that from the time I was a little girl, nothing in my life ever made sense or had any order. I think that's why I had the need to be in control of something. I may not have been able to control my childhood, but I did have a choice in who I would marry, how many children I would have, and ultimately what my life would look like. At least I thought I did. Then I met him ... my first husband. He turned my whole world upside down, and I just couldn't get enough of him. I knew from the day we met that I would love him forever. I didn't realize until it was too late that loving him would ultimately mean that I would have to love myself less.

I met him in high school and instantly fell in love with everything about him, from his walk and the way he talked to his beautiful smile. His teeth were so white, and when he smiled it was like the sun was shining on your face. I would sometimes gaze at him for hours, thinking about how wonderful life with him would be once we got married. We'd have lots of children with at least one boy who would be the mirror image of his father. I knew our little girls would be daddy's girls, because he'd be so good with them and always be a great father. I had it all planned out and knew we'd live happily ever after.

I didn't yet recognize that my gravitation toward him was less about who he was and more about who I wasn't. I didn't possess confidence or self-assurance. I hated myself and everything about me. If I could've erased who I was and started all over, then that would've been my wish. When I met him, I was looking for a way to escape my life. There was so much lacking inside me that I can't honestly say that I could have loved someone else, because I didn't love myself. So, he represented a void I was desperately trying to fill. I was expecting him to do something that he was never meant to do. When he fell short, it was misery for both of us.

When you plan your life and put all the pieces together, but forget to take your plans to God, things often go awry. God already knows who the perfect person is for each of us. He knows who we need to become one with to reach the purpose he has given us, but when we take it into our own hands, we take ourselves off track. This is what I did when I decided that he was the one I would marry. I gave my heart to someone that God knew wasn't the one for me. He was never supposed to be my Prince Charming, but I didn't know it because I was being led by what my heart was telling me.

My wedding day was nothing like I had planned it to be. Instead of having a beautiful white gown, I wore jeans and a t-shirt. We weren't surrounded by all the people who loved us, there were only strangers at a government building who were there to do the same thing as us. The wedding was a quick one, filled with no fanfare or cheers from our mothers and siblings. The ceremony only lasted the amount of time it took us to repeat after the clerk. Then it was over in an instant. We didn't even have rings to exchange. This was supposed to be one of the happiest days of my life, but it ended up being one that I would one day regret. This was not a memory I'd later share with my daughters. At the end of the day, I realized I had given myself to the wrong man. I thought he was my Prince Charming, but he'd quickly taught me that fairy tales weren't real.

Once we were married, we both enlisted in the US Army. Days after that, we were headed to Ft. Bragg,

North Carolina. That was the beginning of our supposedly wonderful life and bright future. Unfortunately, life wouldn't be as wonderful as I had planned. No matter how much I tried to control and orchestrate the steps of my life, I would have very little control over the events that would soon follow, for years to come.

My new husband was no gentleman. He was a wolf in sheep's clothing. There's a saying that people will only show you what they want you to see. The sad thing is that I saw who he was long before we ever uttered the words "I do." He had given me glimpses into his true character long before that dreadful day. I remember the first time he hit me—and every time after that. Memories like that aren't easily forgotten. They make an imprint on your mind the moment they occur and remain there for the rest of your life.

I wanted to be everything he needed me to be; I wanted to please him in every way. I knew that he was at his best when he was happy with me. That was usually when he was able to resist going to the dark place. He only allowed the monster inside him to surface when I wasn't everything he needed of me. If I was the perfect wife, then it would make it easier for him to be a great husband.

I made so many excuses for the way he treated me while at the same time trying to understand why he was a man that I no longer recognized. Each time he exploded, I always reasoned away why he did it or ended up blaming myself. It must've somehow been my fault.

What button did I unknowingly push that ignited the fire inside him? If I could just figure out the answer to that question, then I'd know how to solve this problem we kept having. The fights went from happening infrequently to an almost daily occurrence. It was getting harder for me to justify his behavior. I could no longer pretend that this was normal or that our life was perfect. It was time to take off the rose-colored glasses.

When you live with a certain façade for so long, you begin to believe in the lies you tell other people. It's no longer just about hiding the truth from them, but also hiding it from yourself. It's easier to live a world of make-believe if you're constantly overlooking what's in front of you. We lived in this crazy cycle of fights, break-ups, and getting back together for years. I thought life would get better once we started having babies, but it went from bad to worse. There were trips to the hospital, times when the police were called, and even days when he'd kick the kids and me out of the home we shared. I could do nothing right and everything I said was wrong. He didn't care that our children were afraid of him. The constant look of fear in their eyes didn't disturb him as much as it should have.

This ugly cycle continued for the duration of our marriage. Then one day I realized that I couldn't take it anymore. I had to get myself and my children out of this hell we were living in. Sadly, it wasn't because of his abuse, but the fact that he had chosen to dishonor and abuse me in other ways. He didn't just show his contempt for me with his fists, he showed it in his actions as well. He had little regard for the sanctity of our marriage. Every time he left our home to be with another woman, he was telling me that he hated me to his core and wanted to hurt me in every way possible. What did I do to this man that made him want to destroy me? I didn't understand why the cheating was the thing that pushed me over the edge, but it was what I needed to open my eyes to see the "real" him. Why is it that I saw him being with other women as more of a betrayal than his putting his hands on me to inflict pain? Sometimes it's hard to understand what motivates us to do what is best for our survival.

He had hurt me, he had hurt my children, but it wasn't until he gave himself to other women that I realized that maybe I could do better. I had allowed this man to take everything from me, including my self-respect. I'd spent so many years trying to be what he needed me to be that I forgot to be who God created me to be. It was time for me to stop ignoring my responsibility to myself and my children. I had to draw on the strength I didn't know existed inside me to do something different.

He had always told me that no one else would want me. He made sure I knew how lucky I was to be with him. He chose me! The sad thing is . . . I believed every word he said. Where would I ever find someone to love me like he did? Who would want a woman with three children? Despite these ugly thoughts running through my mind, I knew I had to get out. I couldn't allow his words to manipulate me any longer. I got out and never looked back.

That's how the story should've ended, but it didn't. The sad truth is that we reconnected, and I remarried him a little over four years later. Why would I go backward instead of continuing to move forward in my life? I already knew who he really was, so how could I place myself and my children back into this detrimental situation? There were three things that motivated me to return to him. At the time I didn't realize what those things were, but I've had many years since then to reflect on them. I had to do so to make real changes in my life, so I could break the cycle in my life and in the lives of my children.

First, my parents divorced when I was a little girl and I always secretly wished that they would get back together. I grew up wanting our family to look like that of my friends . . . whole and complete with a mommy and a daddy. I was always looking for what I thought I missed out on, and I wanted to make sure my own children didn't have the same regrets. I realized later that this was one of the driving forces that caused me to talk this man into marrying me again. Yes, I talked him into rekindling our relationship. I thought it was what my children needed if they were going to be who they were supposed to be in this life.

The second dominating factor was that after we left him the first time, I deceived myself into thinking I didn't need counseling to help me heal from the years of abuse that had been inflicted upon me. In my mind, it was okay to just move on and not revisit the things that had happened. I thought that it was too much pain to revisit and that time would heal my wounds. The lies we tell ourselves are the most detrimental to our growth. We can't successfully accomplish everything we're destined to do if we keep tripping over our past hurts. Instead of taking the time to heal and find out how I had allowed myself to be beaten down, I continued moving through life as if the abuse had never happened to me. God has a way of making us deal with things, even when we try to run away from them.

The final thing that caused me to make the same mistake twice was the fact that I had lived with self-loathing for most of my life. It wasn't because my daddy didn't tell me I was pretty or because I didn't have a relationship with him. Instead, it was the many abuses I had endured during my childhood. By the time I met my first husband I was already damaged. I was primed and ready for him to continue what I was used to getting. How he treated me was exactly how I thought I deserved to be treated. I didn't feel worthy of anything more. Therefore, it was so easy for him to mold me into what he wanted and needed.

The abuse in our second marriage would again last for its duration before I had the courage to leave and NEVER look back. This time was different because I knew who I was. I had come into an encounter with our heavenly Father and I knew that I was beautifully and wonderfully made. My abuser could no longer tell me that I was trash or that I was worth nothing because God told me I was the apple of his eye.

The pivotal thing that told me it was time to leave was the way he treated our children. They were property to him instead of his legacy. I began to see the same horror in their eyes that I saw in my own, and I knew I had to save them from this life, even if it meant they would be separated from their father. But then, in his ultimate act of betrayal, he made the decision that if he couldn't have me, then no one would. Not even our children! My husband had every intention of killing me that night, but God had a different plan. Had it not been for God saving my life that dreadful night, I wouldn't be here today to tell my story.

Up until that moment I had lived my life with him as my focus. Now it was finally time to make a permanent change, to live the abundant life that God said I had access to. It was time to focus on God, my children, and myself. In those final days of waiting to get my children and me to a safe place, God showed me so many things he had waiting for me. He gave me glimpses of my destiny, which included me ministering to thousands of women. I learned to lean heavily on the guiding of the Holy Spirit because I knew I needed God to help me heal and be set free from the chains that had bound me for so many years. Jeremiah 29:11 says, "For I know the plans I have for you, declares the Lord, plans to prosper you and not to harm you, plans to give you hope and a future." I clung to this verse daily. It was what helped me through so many days when I struggled with believing God was with me.

Once we left my husband, there were so many things I had to do for us to be whole again. We were homeless, and I had no job. Since we were in Germany when the assault occurred, we came back to the United States with nothing. For the next six or eight months, I worked two jobs while I saved money to get us a permanent home. During that time, we lived in a Sunday School classroom that was part of our church. There were many difficult days, but I knew God was with us.

This time around, I knew the importance of giving myself time to heal. I couldn't allow myself to go into another relationship without loving myself and knowing who God said I was. There were times when I was tempted to forego the process, but I knew I had to push through the pain to get my healing. During the years after, I focused on strengthening my relationship with my heavenly Father. I also devoted my time to the care of my children and helping them overcome the obstacles they faced in their healing process. It was just us, and that was exactly what it needed to be.

God often gives us sweet gifts when we least expect them. This is what he did when he brought my current husband into my life. I had spent years telling God I didn't want to be married again. I felt it was enough for me to raise my children and see them happy. I didn't believe there was a happy ending or a happily ever after for me. Sometimes we think that we've made too many mistakes and don't deserve God's best. Thankfully, God loves us so much that he gives us second, third, and fourth chances, even when we don't deserve them. Revelation 21:5b says, "Behold, I make all things new." When God looked at me, he didn't see all the bad choices of my past. He saw a beautiful bride that he had prepared for the one after his own heart.

There were so many questions I asked myself while courting my current husband. What if this was a mistake? How could I know for sure he wouldn't hurt me? Would he be able to love my children through their hurts? How would my children react to me having someone in my life? The questions went on and on, but at the end of the day I knew this was the man God had prepared for me. It didn't matter that I had messed up so many times before, because God had wiped the slate clean. Ecclesiastes 3:11a says, "He hath made everything beautiful in his time." Through days of praying and fasting, I knew that this man was God's will for my life and the lives of my children. When God brings someone into your life, it's not just about you, but also the people the two of you will reach with your unified purpose. God's ultimate purpose for my life included a man who would be one after his own heart; therefore, he would love me as the daughter of the King that I am.

There's a question I've often been asked when people hear my story, and that is, if I could change anything, what would it be? My response is always, I wouldn't change anything. Romans 8:28 says, "And we know that all things work together for good to them that love God, to them who are the called according to his purpose." I believe that everything I've endured in my life, both good and bad, God has turned around for my good. In my renewed purpose after this experience I've learned to trust God as he continues to lead me on this wonderful journey of sharing my story and helping other women gain deliverance and freedom.

# SOS: Struggle, Obsession, and Self-Care
## Ruby Mabry

For as long as I can remember, I was the tall, dark-skinned, shy girl with low self-esteem. This stems all the way back to kindergarten. Back then, the teachers did home visits for parent/teacher conferences, and when my teacher came to our home, she told my parents that I was a very respectful young lady and did well with my school work, but that I did not want to talk. She stated, "If I ask Ruby a question, she does not answer and just looks at me." The teacher wanted to make sure that I was okay and did not have a hearing problem or any other issues. My parents told her that that was just how I was, that I was just a very quiet, reserved, and shy little girl…

It was the summer of 1984 when one of my parents' male friends came to our home to visit our family. I'm from a Caribbean background, and we were raised such that, whenever we had guests come over, we had to come out and greet the guest and ask if they wanted something to drink, and afterward, we were to retreat back into our rooms to let the adults converse. On that day, I came out to say hello and the gentleman looked at me and said, "Wow, look at you," and spun me around. He then proceeded to make up a song and it went like this: "Someone's getting fat, someone with the blue pants on." He smiled. I felt uncomfortable and embarrassed. The way he said it, in my eyes, was very negative. I was only 115 pounds back then. Before that remark from him, I felt that I looked pretty good. I was tall and thin, yet curvy, with long hair and smooth dark skin, just a typical fun-loving teenager. Again, I was just a teenager, and his definition of fat was me having more hips and backside, which is normal for a teenager. As a female gets older, she becomes curvier. I didn't see it that way as a teenager, though. I was crushed by his comments and his judgment. The shy little girl became more withdrawn and newly obsessed with her physical appearance. I was looking in the mirror thirty or forty times a day, being ashamed and disgusted with what I saw. I literally liked when the mirror was a little smudgy, because in my eyes it made me appear thinner. The smudge distorted the correct view. I was trying to figure out what could I do to lose my hips, bottom, thighs, etc. at 115 pounds. Whew! Just thinking about this now is heart wrenching. My weight was already low, and at that tender age I was trying to lower it.

My first diet was at fourteen years old. I was constantly dieting. It was a time in my life where I was overly obsessed about my physical appearance. I did not count calories, but I ate very little, if anything at all. My mother was such a homemaker; when we were younger, she always had a great breakfast prepared for us before school.

As we grew and became teenagers, our parents let go of the reins a bit due to all four kids having different preferences, so she let us fix whatever we wanted to eat for breakfast. As a teenager, I did not eat breakfast before school, and I ate a bag of chips and a drink for lunch at school. My biggest meal was at dinner time, due to the entire family sitting down together for dinner. My lifestyle habit became taking diet pills, an overabundance of them. Looking back, a life-threatening amount of them. I was also taking laxatives and water pills. My thoughts were inappropriate when it came to eating. I truly felt as though if I ate a full meal, I would get so fat. As a teenager, my mindset was distorted. Society places so much emphasis on being thin. We get sucked up in the hype, which makes us in turn dislike what we see.

I had many moments of feeling faint and dizzy in high school. I had been yo-yo dieting since I was fourteen years old. It was a mental thing. I still heard that song in my head: "Someone's getting fat, someone with the blue pants on." No one knew what I was going through. I convinced myself that I had a defective body. There is so much pressure as a teenager.

Over the summer, I started to fill out all over. I remember how, in high school, guys would make perverted remarks and not look at me in the eyes, but instead look at body parts. I didn't like that feeling. I tried to cover my curves with bigger clothing or a large shirt that covered my breasts and backside.

After years of binge dieting in high school, I began passing out. I can clearly remember the first time; we were in class. I was in the school ensemble, a choral group, and we were practicing on the bleachers for an upcoming performance. I suddenly began feeling faint and passed out. One of the other students drove me home. I told my mom I just did not feel good. She made me some tea and told me to go lay down to see if I would feel better after a nap. I had had nothing to eat that day but diet pills.

Throughout the years, I was up in weight and down in weight. It was just a repetitive cycle. When I look at my pictures from the past, I am shocked at the drastic difference. I can tell in each picture when I was happy and when I was sad. In the thinner pictures, I was feeling sick all the time, I was moody, my heart was racing, I had facial breakouts, I had a lack of confidence, I was weak, and I was always on a "diet"—but I had the thigh gap that I wanted. In the pictures where I wasn't as thin, I was happy, I was more confident, I was outgoing, I smiled more, I was healthier, I had clearer skin, etc.

I never thought that I had an eating disorder because in my eyes, I was not vomiting into the toilet. That is because I was not educated or informed about eating disorders.

My family always gave me positive feedback and told me how great I looked. They never made me feel that I was overweight. I sometimes wonder what my poor sister thinks to herself about me, because I always dump my body image issues on her, and she always says, "You are trippin', you look great. People pay to look the way you look." She is always a great encourager.

As I grew older, and my weight continued to go up and down, I realized that food was not my problem; my problem was my personal issues that caused me to emotionally eat and made me feel shame and secrecy regarding food and my body image. My eating came from my emotions, and I realize now that there was an emotional reason this was happening. I self-soothed with food. I was at war with myself, and this lasted for about three years.

After I married, the same pattern continued. I starved myself. My husband would ask, "what did you eat today?" or tell me, "you can't starve yourself," or say, "when you start back to eating, you will gain twice the weight." As a soldier in the Army, he exercised frequently, so he gave me helpful tips on eating properly and we started exercising together. However, my weight still went up and down. I was not overweight, but there was a look I was going for. The thin, model look. It was embedded in my mind. Throughout movies, television, and magazines, that look is the only one that is associated with being beautiful. I remember I would wear too-big clothing to camouflage my derriere. I was just self-conscious about it. When my daughter became older, I had to consciously stop saying anything in front of her regarding my weight to prevent her from being trapped in the same cycle I was in. As she grew older, she would say, "I wish I had your curves, Mommy." I always told her that she had the perfect body. I did not want my daughter growing up with self-image issues. As women, we were not born hating our bodies. This is something that is taught.

After the death of my mother, which was a traumatic loss in my life, I became broken and helpless. I began not eating again and it brought me to a state of depression. People talk about being a functional alcoholic; well, I was a functional depressed woman.

After doing research, I self-diagnosed myself with being an emotional eater and having body dysmorphic disorder. It causes me to fixate on my body imperfections, to obsess about them, and they become the only thing I see when I look in the mirror. These obsessive and controlling thoughts can lead you to believe what people tell you about your looks, conceal the flaw you obsess over, socially withdraw, or even have thoughts of suicide. I am educated, intelligent, and a pretty successful black woman. So I was not sure how to derail my mental state. My desire to be thinner and fit society's mold was literally killing me and affecting my health. I was a slave to my body size. Even if I lost weight, it was never enough. I was spiraling out of control and it had become an uphill battle.

In the last few years, I again started numbing myself with food. People look at me as poised, professional, and perfect, but I am far from it. I am flawed just like everyone else. I am now at the highest weight I have ever been.

When I saw I was at it again and on a diet, I realized what I was doing immediately, so decided to sign myself up for a gym and began eating better and healthier. The more stressed that I am, the more I eat. I had to come to terms with the harm that I was doing to myself and stop the vicious cycle I was in. Needless to say, I took a difficult step and I sought out professional help for this. Having an eating disorder or body dysmorphic disorder is a serious condition that causes feelings of guilt, disgust, anxiety, or depression. It is vital to seek help from a health professional, such as a psychiatrist, therapist, or nutritionist. Having someone else talk to me about my body dysmorphia has helped put my thoughts and feelings about my body into perspective and helped me create distance from the abusive thoughts that have kept me unhealthy for so many years. This has been a tremendous step in my healing process. I am no longer on a quest for perfection. I am on a quest to live a happier and healthier life.

Some of the signs and symptoms that I experienced were overeating, compulsiveness, exercising, and walking by a mirror many times, looking at back fat and stomach rolls, and even though to others it looked normal, in my eyes, it was hideous. I weighed myself constantly, took hours to get ready, and changed clothes sometimes five or six times due to feeling overweight in a particular outfit. I was finding and using new weight loss supplements in search of perfection. I now realize that there is no such thing as perfection.

Never in a million years would I have thought I would be so transparent about my body issues. But I have made peace with this and I feel it is necessary to share this now, because there are so many people battling this issue. I want to ask adults to watch what they are saying to their children or other's children. I made sure when I had my daughter that I never told her she looked fat or needed to lose weight, or anything derogatory. What you tell a child when they are young truly impacts their future. It is important to share our stories to let young ladies and women know that we are all beautiful, no matter what our color, shape, or size. The scale does not define who you are. Your pants size does not define who you are. We need to embrace every part of our body, not just parts of it.

We all have issues and should all be transparent enough to share our stories so we can help someone else who is going through the same thing. We need to realize that our issues are a work in progress and it is possible to do better. Every day for me is a new day. I am not recovered, but I acknowledge that I am a work in progress. I am working hard to change my relationship with food and to share my journey with and empower other women. I am turning my darkest thoughts into a memoir and my pain into purpose.

I made a conscious effort to shift my mindset and heal my body. Self-confidence is truly hard. I continue to take small steps every day and will continue to build up others affected by this. Especially as women, we need to build each other up instead of hating on one another, and we need to just celebrate our strengths and our beauty.

I had to snap out of it, start journaling, and contact a counselor because I felt I would spiral out of control. If you are in a similar situation, I urge you to seek help and begin journaling to break the chains of low self-esteem, lack of confidence, and poor opinions of your body image. It will help you gain more clarity on what is causing your behavior or feelings and give you a whole new outlook and freedom. I ask myself through journaling: what am I struggling with today/this week/this month? What am I obsessing about? What am I doing to improve my self-care? All of these are relevant questions in order to heal and move forward.

In closing, my struggle and my healing has taught me that I am beautiful. I am curvy and that is fine. I am worthy. I am strong. I am victorious. I am more than just a body. I am not my weight and I am not my pants size.

It's okay to be you. It's okay to be different. It's okay to be thick and fine, and it's okay to be transparent and share your flaws with others in hopes of inspiring them, raising awareness, and raising self-esteem.

Know that God's timing is always perfect and that he has a strategic plan for your life. Watch the mental words that you say to yourself because words have creative power. Self-love is always the best love.

# About the Authors

## Cheryl Sharpe

Forty-two-year-old Orlando native Cheryl Sharpe is no stranger to adversity. She has overcome childhood abuse of many forms, survived a broken neck at the age of seventeen, defied death by the age of twenty-five, and is now overcoming lupus.

Cheryl's tenacity and love for life, God, and others has been her motivation to start her own business, Sharpe Beauty & Wellness Spa. It will offer beauty and wellness as a choice for self-preservation, based on the Maslow hierarchy model. The Day Spa has been a vision of Cheryl's for ten years.

Cheryl Sharpe is an established resident of Winter Garden, Florida, a suburb of Orlando. She has been involved in community service for over twenty years. Cheryl is currently a student at Liberty University working on degrees in business, health science, and counseling. Cheryl's life goal is to use her journey to inspire other people.

Please feel free to contact her at
Cheryldsharpe@gmail.com

About the Authors

## Dawn Collins

Dawn Collins currently resides in the Queen City of the South—Charlotte, North Carolina. She holds a bachelor of arts in communication studies and a master's in public administration, and is currently pursuing a doctorate in healthcare administration. Dawn is a project manager in the healthcare industry and is fascinated with the changing technological dynamics in our health system. In her spare time, Dawn enjoys spending time with her family and friends, reading inspirational novels, and exploring exotic destinations with awe-inspiring sunsets and tranquil beaches.

Having experienced many obstacles in her life, Dawn strives daily to live life unapologetically and to never allow her circumstances to define her future. Her personal mission statement is to live a life of balance while continually learning from life's experiences and cultivating a legacy that will inspire others.

Learn more at
info@iamdawncollins.com

# Sabah Bissainthe

Sabah Bissainthe was born and raised in Liberia, West Africa. At the age of twenty-two, she escaped a civil war in the early nineties and eventually made it to America. It was a joyful moment, knowing that she was in the land of opportunity. But the joy was often overshadowed with loneliness and a sense of defeat as she struggled to define herself once again. Her first job in America was at a cafeteria in Decatur, Georgia, where she served cornbread and dinner rolls. Her accent often prompted questions like "where are you from?" or "did you wear regular clothes in Africa?" With determination to rise above her circumstances and resist defeat, she made it through college by working two or three jobs at a time. She earned a bachelor of science degree in nursing in 1998. She is married with two children and currently works as a nurse consultant.

Learn more at
sidriss68@gmail.com

About the Authors

## Marlyn Bonzil-Juste

Marlyn Bonzil-Juste is an entrepreneur with a diversified background in business development, marketing, strategic client development, and project delivery. With an exceptional ability to facilitate cohesive teams, interface with public agencies, and liaise with key stakeholders, Marlyn is known for her remarkable interpersonal skills and kindred spirit.

As the founder and owner of MJ Solutions, LLC, Marlyn and her team have been able to offer a tailored business solutions portfolio to firms within the legal and healthcare industries. She holds a bachelor's degree in business administration and a master's degree in healthcare administration.

Mrs. Bonzil-Juste stands behind her motto: Create Yourself. This has fueled her passion to continually evolve and deepen her found belief in practicing a holistic approach to living. She currently resides with her family in central Florida where she is active in the community at large, with a special focus on the Haitian-Caribbean and African-American markets.

# Muriel Bissainthe

Muriel Bissainthe is an office manager for a cardiology practice and a public relations board member with the Greater Haitian American Chamber of Commerce–Orlando. She has an associate's degree in nursing. She is an inventor, licensed cosmetologist, and model. Muriel is also co-owner of an online retail store. She has three beautiful children and a loving life partner.

Follow her on Instagram:
@Onlymuriel

## Jamila Khechen

Jamila Khechen was born and raised in Dakar, Senegal, in West Africa. In 2001, at the age of twenty, she moved to the United States. She graduated with honors, majoring in biology and chemistry, and was inducted into Phi Theta Kappa. She is a social worker with the Agency for People with Disabilities. She has been a supported living coach for nine years and volunteers at the Veterans Affairs hospital. She also tutors in English, French, and science. She married the love of her life, Max Gracia, a Navy veteran, and has three beautiful children: Nathaniel, Nehemiah, and Ivanna Gracia. She loves spending quality time with her family, listening to music, traveling in the US, and exploring new adventures. Her goal is to write books and give back to the community. Her passion is helping the unfortunate. She would like to continue to encourage other women and young children.

# Tyria D. Jones

Tyria D. Jones was born in Pompano Beach, Florida. She currently resides in Houston with her husband Kenneith and her youngest daughter, Kiara. She and Kenneith have been happily married for six years. She has seven children and five grandbabies. Her life is filled with overflowing joy, but it hasn't always been so happy. She struggled for most of her life trying to find out who God created her to be. What was her purpose in life? What made her special in God's eyes? It wasn't until she started looking at herself the way that God does that she realized she had a story to share and that her purpose was in that story. Tyria has always had a ministry for women; however, it is through the pain that she overcame in her own life that God has allowed her to write her book, *A Crown of Beauty for Ashes*.

Learn more at
www.tyriadjones.com

## Ruby Mabry

Ruby Mabry is an international bestselling author, a thought leader and coach, and the CEO of New Life Manor, Inc. She is a board member of the Greater Haitian American Chamber of Commerce in public relations and marketing, and she is also the founder of the Live on Purpose Movement, where she unites, inspires, and empowers women to live their true purpose in life and in business.

Facebook: Author Ruby Mabry
Instagram: Author Ruby Mabry
Email: AuthorRubyMabry@gmail.com
Website: www.liveonpurposemastermind.com

## CREATING DISTINCTIVE BOOKS WITH INTENTIONAL RESULTS

We're a collaborative group of creative masterminds with a mission to produce high-quality books to position you for monumental success in the marketplace.

Our professional team of writers, editors, designers, and marketing strategists work closely together to ensure that every detail of your book is a clear representation of the message in your writing.

### Want to know more?
Write to us at info@publishyourgift.com
or call (888) 949-6228

Discover great books, exclusive offers, and more at
**www.PublishYourGift.com**

Connect with us on social media

@publishyourgift

www.ingramcontent.com/pod-product-compliance
Lightning Source LLC
Chambersburg PA
CBHW052100070526
44584CB00017B/2263